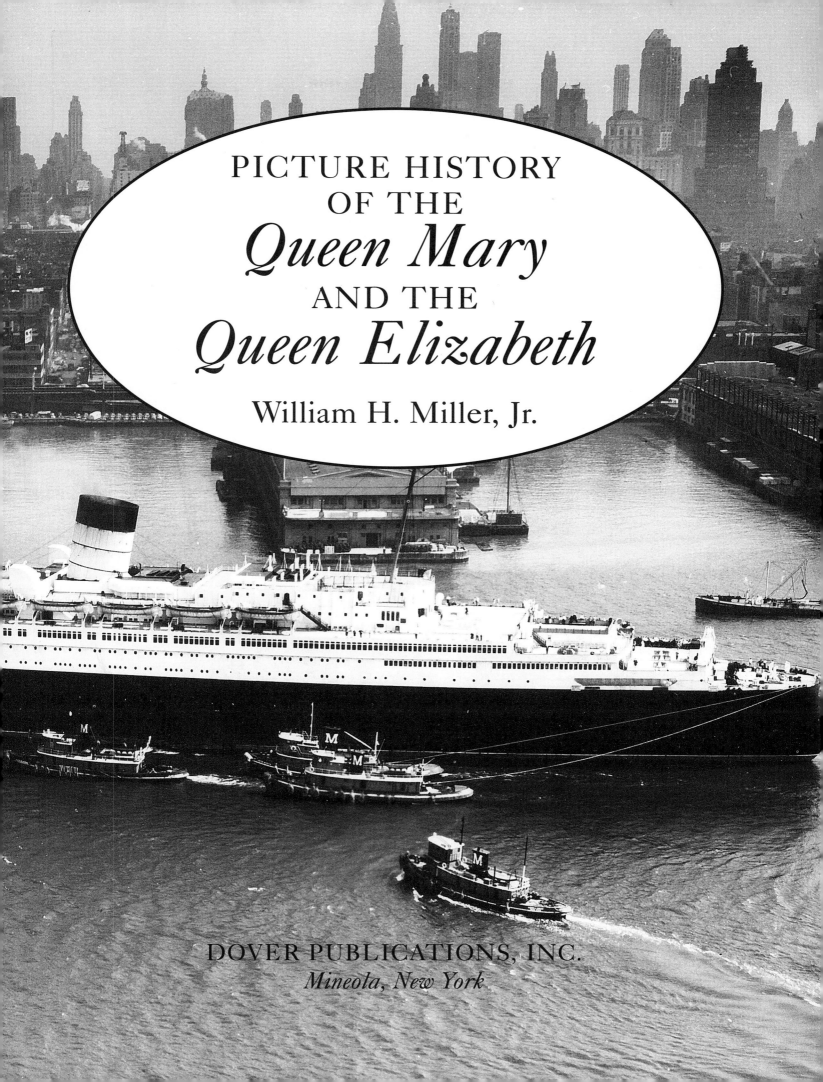

PICTURE HISTORY OF THE
Queen Mary
AND THE
Queen Elizabeth

William H. Miller, Jr.

DOVER PUBLICATIONS, INC.
Mineola, New York

FOR MAURIZIO ELISEO
*A kind, generous, world-class ocean liner
historian, author, and dear friend*

Bibliographical Note

Picture History of the Queen Mary *and the* Queen Elizabeth is a new work, first published by Dover Publications, Inc., in 2004.

Library of Congress Cataloging-in-Publication Data

Miller, William H., 1948–
    Picture history of the Queen Mary and the Queen Elizabeth / William H. Miller.
        p. cm.
    Includes bibliographical references and index.
    ISBN 0-486-43509-1 (pbk.)
    1. Queen Mary (Steamship)—History. 2. Queen Elizabeth (Ship)—History. I. Title.

VM383.Q4M54 2004
387.5'42—dc22

                                                                            2004045548

*Book design by Carol Belanger Grafton
Typesetting by Irene Kupferman*

Manufactured in the United States of America
Dover Publications, Inc., 31 East 2nd Street, Mineola, N.Y. 11501

ACKNOWLEDGEMENTS

Just as it takes many hands to build a ship, creating a book is not a one-person endeavor. As the author, I am merely the coordinator—the chief purser, if you will—of the production. Once a title is selected, it is divided into chapters based on historical reference and chronology, and also on the availability of interesting and reproducible photographs. As many as 90 percent of these images are borrowed by loyal, generous, and very patient friends—the crew, if you will. Descriptions are written, often spiced and enriched with anecdotes and recollections from former staff members, passengers, maritime enthusiasts, and nautical observers. In the end, the completed book is hoped to bring readers on an imaginative voyage, just as ships do.

I am always indebted to the superb Dover Publications, which, in some twenty-five years, has taken on many ocean liner titles. It all began one spring morning in the company's former Varick Street offices in Lower Manhattan, with an informal meeting that included the late Hayward Cirker, founder and owner of Dover. He was an inspiration, a great source of encouragement and support, and a man who loved to document history in almost all forms. Fortunately, he found ocean liners rather interesting, and I could not have been in better hands ever since. Among other reasons, Dover does an impeccable job of using photographs in book form. My best thanks also to Clarence Strowbridge, president of Dover, for continuing my relationship with the company, and to the fine, thorough, very thoughtful and reflective editorial staff, especially Jenny Bak. They always take my manuscripts and make them better, clearer, more readable, and more interesting.

Others who helped with this particular project include Richard Faber, the well-known ocean liner memorabilia dealer and collector. Overly generous, he has been a source of, not only prized photos, but all-important resource materials: books, brochures, menus, and sailing schedules. Very special thanks also to Abe Michaelson, my business partner for over twenty years, who keeps records, handles finances, and sees that these books are sent to the four corners of the globe.

My warmest appreciation as well to Captain Ian McNaught and Maureen Ryan, both from Cunard, for their fine introductory words.

Others deserving of high appreciation include Ernest Arroyo, Frank Braynard, Michael Cassar, Anthony Cooke, Luis Miguel Correia, the late Frank Cronican, Frank Duffy, Maurizio Eliseo, the late John Gillespie, David Hutchings, Norman Knebel, Peter Knego, Sal Scannella, the late Everett Viez, and Al Wilhelmi. My thanks to still others: Frank Andrews, Knut Aune, Philippe Brebant, Stephen Card, Tom Cassidy, Tom Chirby, the late Dianne Coles, Robin Davies, Jerry Davis, Tony Dent, Laurence Dunn, John Ferguson, Kirk Frederick, Nico Guns, Andy Hernandez, Herbert Jaeger, Ray Kane, Philippe Kass, Dewey & Tricia Kennell, Andy Kilk, Captain Reidulf Maalen, Vic Marinelli, Andrew Nelder, Ove Nielsen, Rich Romano, Der Scutt, Don Stoltenberg, Mary Thomas, Dan Trachtenberg, Frank Trumbour, Gordon Turner, David Williams, and Captain Paul Wright. Other kind assistance and support came from Robert Bloch, Peter Chase, Martin Cox, Andrew Dibben, Mitchell Mart, William Muller, Mario Pulice, Thomas Rennesland, and Commodore and Mrs. Ronald Warwick.

Companies, organizations, and even websites that should be noted include Carnival Cruise Lines, Chantiers de l'Atlantique, Cunard Line, Moran Towing & Transportation Company, Ocean Books, Ocean Liner Council at South Street Seaport, Port Authority of New York & New Jersey, Queen Mary Museum, Steamship Historical Society of America (especially the Long Island chapter) and World Ship Society (in particular, the Port of New York and Southampton branches).

FOREWORD I

It is with great pleasure that I put pen to paper to write an introduction for a book about two great ships—and not just any ships, but probably the two most famous liners in the world at the time, *Queen Mary* and *Queen Elizabeth*.

Much has been written about these two liners over the years, and I am sure there is still much more to tell. Both ships have fascinating histories, from their building, maiden voyages, war service, to those glorious days of transatlantic travel after World War II, and finally how Cunard tried to go cruising with the two Atlantic giants in their twilight years before their inevitable end.

As a boy in the 1960s, I can well remember the television and newspaper reports telling us about the final crossings of both ships, and with what great regret all this was reported. It was the end of an era!

Cunard, however, had other plans, a vision that other lines were maybe not brave enough to grasp, and so the concept of *QE2* came into being—a transatlantic liner that could also go cruising. I can still recall that day in September 1967, as a thirteen-year-old boy, lying on the floor watching the televised footage of Her Majesty Queen Elizabeth II naming and launching this great ship. And now here I am, some thirty-six years later, sailing her as Master, and very proud to be part of Cunard history.

Times move on and things change, and now Cunard is part of Carnival Corporation and we are moving into the twenty-first century with another great liner on the horizon, *Queen Mary 2*.

QM2 will be, at the time of her maiden voyage in January 2004, the largest liner ever built and will sail in the wake of her predecessors as a trendsetter for the rest of the industry to follow in the great traditions of transatlantic liners.

CAPTAIN IAN MCNAUGHT
Master, *Queen Elizabeth 2*
May 2003

FOREWORD II

The date was January 7, 2002. The time: 6:20 A.M.

In the bleak darkness and sleet, the *QE2* moved closer to Manhattan, the Statue of Liberty and, slowing gradually, passed the Battery. Shortly after, as the first morning light started to break, the ship's engines ceased and all was still.

I started out across the bow, my eyes drawn to just one spot, looking to identify the exact location. There it was—huge floodlights illuminating the gap, the void, the hideous open space that was Ground Zero. For so many hundreds of us out on deck that bitterly cold morning, this was the true reality. Forget the TV, the newspapers, the thousands of words written, we were actually here, back in this city, looking out at the devastation.

In another life, it seemed to me, two pinnacles of strength, two gleaming icons of power, soaring towards the sky, glinting in the sun, had stood on that spot. And over the years, the passengers and crew of the *QE2* had gazed in wonder at these remarkable buildings, the World Trade Center towers. Now they were gathered again, this time to stare in sadness.

I waited on the fo'c'sle, holding the wreath, symbol of respect, as the hymn "Amazing Grace" was played, the notes floating over a silent deck. The music ended, and I moved forward, up the deck, accompanied by a navigation officer. Behind me, on every inch of space, hundreds of passengers and crew watched in the drizzle and light snow.

I was conscious only of slight sounds—the sounds of muffled sighs and sobs—as I cast the wreath into the Hudson River in remembrance of all those who lost their lives on that date that is etched onto the pages of history: September 11, 2001. I stepped back, bowed, and the Ensign flag was lowered to half-mast.

Then, into the darkness, the *QE2*'s whistle blew three times, announcing our return to this amazing city—the first cruise ship to return to the Port of New York on a scheduled visit since that terrible day. As the mighty whistle blasted across the water, we were saluting New York City and New Yorkers for their bravery and determination.

The fireboats moved in to escort us up to our berth, as they have escorted Cunarders on so many occasions: the magnificent *Queen Mary* entering New York on her maiden voyage in 1936, her running mate *Queen Elizabeth* arriving in 1940 after a dangerous, secret wartime dash across the Atlantic, and the unique *QE2* sailing to New York so proudly in 1969.

And now we were arriving again, in the dawn of a winter's morning, as the sky brightened over Manhattan. We saw our return as a triumphant new beginning, a signal to the world that good had overcome evil, and a tribute to the enduring spirit of New York City and its people.

MAUREEN RYAN
Social Hostess
Queen Elizabeth 2
May 2003

Maureen Ryan has been sailing with Cunard for some forty years, beginning in 1963 aboard the *Queen Mary* and *Queen Elizabeth*. Onboard *QE2* in 2003, she was said to be the most senior staff member.

PICTURE CREDITS

INTRODUCTION

It seems especially fitting that this book is being created in the year 2003. The Cunard Line—that cherished, all-important, thoroughly historic shipping company—is soon to reach another zenith. Just six months away from delivery as I write this, the 150,000-ton *Queen Mary 2* will be the largest liner ever built, in herself a great revival to the transatlantic passenger ship trade and the flagship of the illustrious Cunard company. She's also the costliest ever built, one of the most powerful and, quite expectedly, a ship of considerable note—those prized statistics and details that passenger line public relations and advertising departments so love. Indeed, she is the most important news-making passenger liner in recent times. And as this brilliant new ship, already dubbed *QM2*, is being readied in the final months of her creation, the age of the Queens will continue. In the spring of 2003, Cunard also announced that a second, brand-new liner—although slightly smaller at 85,000 tons—would be named *Queen Victoria* in time for her delivery in 2005. By then, Cunard would have three superliners: *Queen Mary 2*, *Queen Victoria*, and the *Queen Elizabeth 2*. In April 2004, however, plans suddenly changed. The intended *Queen Victoria* was reassigned by the Carnival Corporation, the parent of Cunard since 1998, to another division, P&O Cruises, to sail as the *Arcadia*. Cunard will build instead a new *Queen Victoria*, also 85,000 tons, scheduled for delivery in 2007. What a collection of impeccable ocean liners! But to many, the greatest ships—in perhaps Cunard's grandest phase—were the original *Queen Mary* and *Queen Elizabeth*. This title highlights these two maritime icons, but it is also a salute—and yet another gala review—of Cunard and its superb passenger ships, especially those of the last seventy years or so.

Back in the 1950s, in my formative years of learning to love the great liners, Cunard was to me rather unique: it was the only big passenger firm to occupy two entire piers along New York City's crowded, very busy "Luxury Liner Row." Passenger shipping was still brisk in those days, both across the Atlantic and to ports in almost every corner of the globe, such that many smaller companies could not even lease a single pier in that prestigious midtown quarter, and so had to use dock space in less convenient, certainly less fashionable locations like lower Manhattan, New Jersey, and even in remote Brooklyn. But Cunard needed those two piers—they had more "big ship" arrivals and sailings than anyone else did. Often, there might be four "Cunarders," as they were fondly called, berthed together. The collection of them, and especially the sight of their orange-red and black funnels, was a feast for the eyes and excitement for the soul.

Cunard occupied Piers 90 and 92: twin 1,100-foot-long finger piers located along the otherwise industrial and tenement-filled West Side, at the foot of 50th and 52nd streets. They were built back in the mid-1930s purposely for the forthcoming arrivals of the two new Queens and for the Italian Line's giants *Rex* and *Conte di Savoia*. Adjacent Pier 88 was created especially for the visits of Cunard's archrival, the new French *Normandie*. It was the high-water era of the transocean superliners—mighty and fast and assuredly glamorous—and Cunard produced two of the very best of the ships—the regal, utterly majestic *Queen Mary* in 1936, and the slightly bigger, slightly more handsome *Queen Elizabeth* four years later. To this day, their legends persist in people's memories and imaginations. The *Mary* lives on, of course, as a permanent museum to the age of the great luxury liners in her southern Californian retirement.

In New York, the comings and goings of the Cunarders could almost be plotted. The Queens almost always arrived on Tuesdays, inbound from Southampton and Cherbourg, and then sailed out the following day. But just in case, you could always check with the "Shipping Mails," the daily shipping schedules that appeared in both the *Herald Tribune* and the *New York Times*. Those mammoth Queens, with their sensitive thirty-nine-foot drafts, had to move according to the Hudson's tidal changes. Therefore, the actual times of their movements changed from week to week. There were, for example, early morning and midday departures, but also late afternoons and even early evening send-offs. I even recall a midnight sailing for the *Elizabeth*. But whatever the hour or weather, the sight of them was always worth the wait—it was pure magic. Towering above the tugs and other assorted harbor craft, they seemed—at least from my front-row seat on the opposite Jersey shoreline—to almost blot out nearly the entire extraordinary New York City skyline. Only skyscrapers such as the Empire State, Chrysler, and RCA buildings seem to peer above from behind. As they serenely but purposely sailed southward along the Hudson, they were very much the grand maritime queens in procession, with the other craft creating the royal court entourage. Sometimes, a friend and I would feel adventurous and together we might go to the rooftop of one of the Hoboken tenements and patiently but excitedly wait for one of the Queens to pass by. The top decks, funnels, and the raked masts seemed to rest on those buildings nearer to the shore, with no sign of under works or hull.

In the 1950s, the Queens always used the north slip of Pier 90. It was reserved for them only and constructed to allow them easy and efficient departures (the stern being swung northwards in the river, for example, and then the ship "straightened" by the assisting tugs for the passage along the Hudson, out to the lower bay, and finally to the Atlantic itself). Cunard's two other big ships had less of a prescribed pattern. The twin-funneled *Mauretania*, certainly one of the most handsome looking liners of her day, and the all-green *Caronia*, which was especially elusive as she was often away on long, luxurious cruises, came and went irregularly and so varied in their use of the piers.

The squattish *Britannic*, last of the old White Star liners and still bearing their funnel colors, tended to almost always use the north side of Pier 92. Despite being some 27,000 tons, she was so flat that she often appeared to be hidden. She shared that berth with two solid-looking, combination passenger-cargo ships, the sisters *Media* and *Parthia*. These two ships usually arrived on Saturdays and, after five or six days of unloading and reloading, sailed again on Thursdays or Fridays. I often recall one of them departing on a Friday afternoon, in fact the busiest period for New York harbor ship departures in those active days. Company accountants wanted their ships out and on their way to avoid being charged expensive weekend-dockers' overtime. The *Media* and *Parthia* also appeared to be, in ways, the busiest Cunard passenger ships at berth. Because they carried considerable cargo (as well as guests), a series of barges were often nested along their outer side, often in company with one or two floating cranes, sometimes one of the muscular, heavy-lift type, as well as railway carfloats.

From December through April, we would see Cunard's diverted Canadian quartet: the dome-funneled *Saxonia, Ivernia, Carinthia,* and *Sylvania.* They, too, would have an extended five or six days in port, coming off the ice-clogged St. Lawrence River service to Montreal and Quebec City. And, of course, there were also Cunard freighters, now something of a forgotten fleet within the company's otherwise luxurious ocean liner image. These cargo ships included the likes of the twin-funneled sister ships *Alsatia* and *Andria,* and members of the more standardized *Asia* class. By the 1960s, however, Cunard seemed to rely more and more on chartered, foreign-flag freighters—Danes, Norwegians, and even a small Dutch combination passenger-cargo ship, the *Prinses Irene,* which assisted on the "whiskey run" from Glasgow.

At the end of most summer vacations from school, I would journey across the lower Hudson to one of the greatest "temples" of so-called "Steamship Row,"—the Cunard Building at 25 Broadway. After gazing at the spectacular model collection (including the four-funneled *Mauretania,* the *Majestic,* and, of course, both of the Queens), I would collect company literature: elaborate booklets, glossy brochures, neatly folded deck plans, and, most particularly, those freshly-issued, orange-colored sailing schedules for the following year.

Those schedules revealed curiously fascinating variations in the otherwise established Cunard sailing patterns. The New York express run, for example, would become more irregular in the slack winter months, especially with the Queens going in for their long overhauls at Southampton. This also meant changes in the fixed pattern, such as having the *Queen Mary* depart on a Saturday instead of the customary Wednesday. It wouldn't be until March or April before the glorious team of the *Mary* and the *Elizabeth* would be back together again in their established rotation.

There would other deviations as well in the sailing patterns. The *Mauretania,* for example, traditionally spent her winters in the Caribbean. Therefore, she tended to sail more frequently from New York, on twelve- to sixteen-day voyages to such sun-drenched destinations as Nassau, Port-au-Prince, Kingston, and—as I recall—even Havana. Each January, the *Britannic* would head off for two months around the Mediterranean and Black Seas on a long, expensive, clublike trip to the Holy Land, the Aegean, the Crimea, and the French Riviera. And, of course, the ultra-luxurious *Caronia* would begin another annual program of extraordinary itineraries. She usually began in January with a ninety-five-or-so day trip around the world (due to the many annual repeat passengers, the itinerary constantly changed in order to visit different ports each year). As the beloved "Green Goddess," she seemed to go just about everywhere: Rio and Capetown, Sydney and Hong Kong, Honolulu and Pago Pago, with more exotic destinations like the Straits of Magellan and the Great Barrier Reef. As a child, I would study the sailing schedule and plan which New York departures I hoped to watch.

Regrettably, I did not actually visit as many Cunarders as I would have liked. Today's high security, absolutely-no-visitors policies were unknown then; I simply paid fifty cents to go aboard and explore the outgoing ships for as long as three hours. From those visits, I recall the comfortable charm of the *Britannic* and the coziness of the little *Parthia.* I remember the *Carinthia's* dining chairs (which had come from the old *Aquitania*), and the etched glass panels and the burl woods of the *Caronia.* I did pay several visits to the Queens, but only in the twilight years (1966–67), by which time they had become museum pieces—Art Deco had yet to be the cherished decorative form it is today.

On a Saturday in November 1963 (in fact, the day after the assassination of President John F. Kennedy), Cunard announced that they were cutting back: in the future, only one passenger pier at New York would be sufficient to their needs. Hereafter, the Italian Line would lease Pier 90. It was certainly a sign of the times, at least for Cunard. The transatlantic passenger trade was fading, passenger rosters had dropped, and even the company's financial state wasn't what it used to be. A few years later, in 1967 and 1968, I would be among those mournful onlookers seeing the *Queen Mary* and then the *Queen Elizabeth* off on their last trips. Briefly, in 1969, it seemed as if a new age had dawned with the spirited welcome for the *Queen Elizabeth 2.* Otherwise, it seemed that the likes of the *Mauretania, Caronia,* and the *Saxonia* quartet had all disappeared with barely any notice. They might just as well have sailed into a shroud of fog. Quite suddenly, by 1969, Cunard was down to only two ships in New York service: the *QE2* running transatlantic crossings, and the restyled *Franconia* offering seasonal, week-long cruises to Bermuda and back.

Cunard's two piers were gutted and then rebuilt in 1973–74, and later became part of Manhattan's new, combined passenger ship terminal. Subsequent Cunarders would visit, including the *Sagafjord, Vistafjord,* and the diminutive *Cunard Princess,* and I would watch them sail as well, though it was not quite the same. The pure excitement of an ocean liner departure had lessened . . . there are no crowds of well-wishers along the dockside, no masses of festive paper streamers, and even the ship's whistles seemed muted.

But the overall effect was still the same—an enormous, luxurious ship heading off to romantic, faraway shores. It is all part of the absolute magic of man harnessing the sea. For me, it prompts memories of ships and sailing days long past, those busy times at Piers 90 and 92, and perhaps of a single afternoon when the *Queen Mary,* the *Mauretania,* the *Caronia,* and the *Media* might have nestled together at berth. What cherished, indelible memories! Perhaps in this book, those great Cunarders, especially the *Queen Mary* and *Queen Elizabeth,* will sail once more.

BILL MILLER
Hoboken, New Jersey
Summer 2003

CONTENTS

CHAPTER I
MARITIME RIVALRY / 1

CHAPTER II
ROYAL DEBUT / 15

CHAPTER III
THE QUEENS AT WAR / 34

CHAPTER IV
GETTING THERE WAS HALF THE FUN / 48

CHAPTER V
DECLINE, WITHDRAWAL, AND A NEW CUNARD / 81

CHAPTER VI
ROYAL SUCCESSORS: QUEEN ELIZABETH 2
AND QUEEN MARY 2 / 96

BIBLIOGRAPHY / 114

INDEX OF SHIPS / 115

MARITIME RIVALRY

The history of the Cunard Line, or the Cunard Steam-Ship Company, Limited, as it was once more formally known, is practically the history of the old North Atlantic passenger service itself. Cunard dominated, competed, innovated, and certainly built some of the most significant passenger ships of all time. They began with a 200-foot-long paddle steamer in the nineteenth century, and now own the 1,132-foot-long *Queen Mary* 2, the largest ocean liner of all time.

Celebrating their 165th anniversary in 2005, Cunard was started in 1839 by a Nova Scotian shipowner, Samuel Cunard. Together with three partners, he luckily obtained the prized mail contract to America from the British Admiralty. The stage was set: he ordered no less than four new packet steamers, and the first of these, the 1,100-ton *Britannia*, sailed from Liverpool to Boston in July 1840. The crossing took fourteen days. The Cunard Line was in business.

By 1900, Cunard transatlantic service, sailing to New York, Boston, and Eastern Canada, were both popular and profitable. Cunard ships were known for their reliability, punctuality, and splendid service. Also, Cunarders (as they were called), seemed always to be in the news as the recipients of acclaim and notation. It was aboard the *Lucania* in 1901, for example, that Marconi carried out his first practical experiments with wireless telegraphy. Two years later, the same ship published the first onboard passenger newspaper carrying daily wireless reports. Another Cunarder, the *Carpathia*, achieved something close to maritime immortality as the principal rescue ship for the passengers of the *Titanic* in April 1912.

In 1905, Cunard introduced two of the biggest and grandest liners then afloat: the 20,000-ton sisters *Carmania* and *Caronia*. Soon afterward, in 1907, Cunard's built two of the world's most spectacular superliners, the 32,000-ton *Mauretania* and *Lusitania*. 1913 welcomed a bigger and more luxurious ship in the form of the 48,000-ton *Aquitania*.

It was in the 1930s, however, that Cunard produced two of its most extraordinary vessels, the incomparable 81,000-ton *Queen Mary* and then the 83,000-ton *Queen Elizabeth*. They ran the world's first weekly, two-ship service across the Atlantic and proved to be, at least for most of their careers, the most successful pair of liners yet built. Their successor, the 65,000-ton *Queen Elizabeth 2*, was added in 1969, and then, biggest of all, the 150,000-ton *Queen Mary* 2 had her debut in 2004.

Cruising has also been an important part of Cunard, including the first, complete around-the-world cruise in 1922 onboard the *Laconia*. Later, in 1948, Cunard built the very first big liner for full-time luxury cruising, the 34,000-ton "second" *Caronia*. Owned by Miami-headquartered Carnival Cruise Lines since 1998, Cunard has been revitalized with the likes of the *Queen Mary* 2 and the addition of the 85,000-ton *Queen Victoria* in 2007. That distinguished corporate name continues as proudly as ever.

In the mid-1930s, Cunard merged with its long-standing rival, the White Star Line, and prepared for the delivery of the record-breaking *Queen Mary*. While the numbers of passengers on the Atlantic had certainly declined in those otherwise lean Depression years, Cunard was running six of the world's most prestigious, largest, and assuredly most luxurious ocean liners: *Mauretania*, *Aquitania*, and *Berengaria*, along with the *Majestic*, *Olympic*, and *Homeric*. No other company could quite compare with Cunard. But though they were large, well decorated, and had their loyal passengers, those six big liners under the new Cunard–White Star house flag were aging and dated. They were becoming less competition to the likes of the French and the Germans, all of whom had or were planning far newer ships. The *Mauretania*, for example, dated from 1907, and had reached old age for an ocean liner by the mid-1930s. Consequently, plans were in place by the late 1920s for the new *Queen Mary*, which was hoped to reestablish Cunard's prominent position on the lucrative but fiercely competitive North Atlantic run. The prestige of the company, as well as of Britain herself, rested in the balance.

CARMANIA. By the turn of the century, competition on the North Atlantic was intensifying at a furious pace. Cunard was not only struggling to compete with the new luxury ships of Britain's White Star Line, but also across the North Sea with the Germans, namely the Hamburg America Line and the North German Lloyd. In response, Cunard laid plans for bigger, better, more notable ships. While designing a particularly handsome pair of twin-stackers—ships that in fact would be nicknamed "the Pretty Sisters"—Cunard engineers became intrigued with the new concept of steam turbine drive. It was said to be an improvement over the steam reciprocating system, which was not only less efficient, but often dirty as well. And so, the company opted to experiment by outfitting the *Carmania* with the steam turbine system and the *Caronia* with the standard reciprocating steam engines. In comparison tests, the *Carmania* proved faster, smoother riding, and far more economical, and so opened a whole new era in ocean liner propulsion. Thereafter, almost all other passenger ships were constructed according to the *Carmania*'s innovation. In the lean years of the early Depression, the twins were used as cruise ships for $50 weeklong trips between New York and Havana, but their long, hardworking careers finally ended in 1932. The *Carmania*, seen here (*opposite, top*), on November 20, 1932, is being stripped of her art treasures and other passenger finery at the Tilbury Docks in London before proceeding to the ship breakers in Scotland. The *Caronia*'s final voyage brought her to Japan, where she was demolished. [Built by John Brown & Company Limited, Clydebank, Scotland, 1905. 19,524 gross tons; 675 feet long; 72 feet wide. Steam turbines, triple screw. Service speed 18 knots. 2,650 passengers as built (300 first-class, 350 second-class, 900 third-class, 1,100 steerage).]

LUSITANIA. The *Carmania* and *Caronia* were, in ways, preludes to bigger, faster, more lavish Cunarders—superliners that could surpass the big German passenger ships. The British government was happy to assist with construction subsidies and operating contracts, especially for mail to and from America, especially after White Star was bought out by J. P. Morgan, the New York–based financier. London ministers wanted British-owned liners to carry the nation's colors, enhance national prestige, and, in case of war, be available for military purposes. The *Lusitania* (*above*), her profile dominated by four tall smokestacks, arrived first in September 1907. She made news rather expectedly on both sides of the Atlantic and was an instant success. The interested public was informed, for example, that she was more than three New York City blocks in length, had three million turbine plates, 192 furnaces, and consumed a thousand tons of coal per day. She could reach as much as 25 knots for her six-day passages between New York and Liverpool. Inside, she was every inch one of the world's "floating palaces," with gleaming marble and polished woods, stained glass skylights, and potted palm verandas. Unfortunately, she came to a tragic end on May 7, 1915. While steaming for Liverpool, she was torpedoed by a German U-boat off southwestern Ireland. Onboard, 1,198 perished out of a total of 1,959 passengers and crew. Considered the worst ocean liner tragedy of the First World War, her sinking, along with other events, gradually drew neutral America into the conflict against the German Kaiser's forces. [Built by John Brown & Company Limited, Clydebank, Scotland, 1907. 31,550 gross tons; 787 feet long; 87 feet wide. Steam turbines, quadruple screw. Service speed 25 knots. 2,165 passengers (563 first-class, 464 second-class, 1,138 third-class).]

MAURETANIA. The *Mauretania* was commissioned two months after its cousin, the *Lusitania*, in November 1907. She took the Blue Riband for the speediest transatlantic crossing, earning her the distinction of the world's fastest liner until 1929, with the arrival of Germany's brand new *Bremen*. The *Mauretania* was not only always more prestigious than the *Lusitania*, but more popular and beloved. She endeared herself to the traveling public, as well as to onlookers, harbor crews, and steamer enthusiasts. Her luxurious appointments had a more "Continental" tone, which included Italian Renaissance and French influences. For her first-class library alone, 300 wood-carvers were brought from Palestine to create the wood paneling and carving. Unlike the *Lusitania*, the *Mauretania* also had a long, largely successful career. After serving as a valiant troopship in the First World War, she resumed Atlantic liner service, teamed with the *Aquitania* and the newly acquired *Berengaria* as part of Cunard's "Big Three." The *Mauretania* is seen here on October 27, 1932 (*opposite, bottom*), docking at the so-called New Docks at Southampton, a brand new facility at the port of Southampton. The *Mauretania* was the first liner to use the berths for a winter overhaul. [Built by Swan, Hunter & Wigham Richardson Limited, Newcastle, England, 1907. 31,938 gross tons; 790 feet long; 88 feet wide. Steam turbines, quadruple screw. 2,335 passengers as built (560 first-class, 475 second-class, 1,300 third-class).]

Even though Cunard was planning a new superliner in 1929 ("a ship exceeding 60,000 tons," as they reported), the Atlantic passenger trade soon faced lean times. Following the Wall Street crash of October 1929, travel began to slump badly. One million voyagers sailed to Europe in 1930, but the number had dropped to 500,000 by 1935. Even Cunarders were sailing at less than capacity. Sailings to and from British ports were reduced, but to avoid lay-up for their liners, some were pressed into still-affordable, short-cruise service. Beginning in 1930, the venerable *Mauretania* (**above**) began spending more and more time on short trips to Bermuda, Nassau, Havana, and even on long weekends up to Halifax, Nova Scotia. A five-day summer trip to Bermuda was priced from $45, but far less costly and therefore more popular were overnight "cruises to nowhere," which had rates beginning at $10 per person. Still caught in Prohibition, the bars on ships such as the British-registered *Mauretania* could be legally opened once at sea, and so thirsty Americans were free to once again enjoy their libations. Dubbed "booze cruises," these voyages were immensely popular and actually saved ships such as the *Mauretania* from premature sailings to the scrappers. To enhance her all-cruising role, the veteran four-stacker was repainted white in 1932. It not only made her seem more tropical, but actually kept her interior as much as ten degrees cooler.

AQUITANIA. Following the enormous success of the *Lusitania* and the *Mauretania* since 1907, Cunard had but a few years before they had to compete with bigger, faster, and certainly more luxurious liners. White Star Line, for example, added no less than three large liners: the 46,000-ton *Olympic* in 1911, *Titanic* a year later, and—bigger still—the 48,000-ton *Gigantic* (later renamed *Britannic*) in 1914. But the Germans, namely the mighty Hamburg America Line, had even more ambitious plans: the 52,000-ton *Imperator* for 1913, the 54,000-ton *Vaterland* for the following year, and then, capping off the trio, the 56,000-ton *Bismarck* in 1914. Cunard, already needing a third big liner to cover a weekly service route between Liverpool and New York, had to respond and reaffirm its position. The result was the 45,000-ton *Aquitania*, which, while not the fastest or even the largest, was acclaimed for her beauty, both inside and out. Soon after her completion in the spring of 1914, she was fondly dubbed "the Ship Beautiful." She, too, did heroic duty in World War I, then returned to Cunard's express service, which had been changed from Liverpool to Southampton by 1920. An enduring ship, also known as the "Grand Old *Aquitania*" in her later years, she was scheduled for well-deserved retirement in 1940, just as the new *Queen Elizabeth* was to join the *Queen Mary*. But when World War II started in September 1939, those plans were shelved as the *Aquitania* was sent to serve as trooper in another war. She even returned to Cunard passenger service before going to the scrappers in 1950. By then, she was the last of the Edwardian "floating palaces," and the last of the great four-stackers. She is seen here (*below*) in the early evening of August 30, 1939, leaving New York's Pier 90 for what would be her final eastbound sailing before the war in Europe officially started on September 3. [Built by John Brown & Company Limited, Clydebank, Scotland, 1914. 45,647 gross tons; 901 feet long; 97 feet wide. Steam turbines, quadruple screw. Service speed 23 knots. 3,230 passengers as built (618 first-class, 614 second-class, 1,998 third-class).]

Considered by many to be one of the most splendid of all Atlantic liners, the *Aquitania* indeed had many beautiful features. Here we see some of her more palatial spaces: the first-class smoking room (*above*), Garden Lounge (*opposite, top*), the main staircase and foyer (*opposite, middle*), and swimming pool with adjoining gymnasium (*opposite, bottom*).

SAMARIA. Following World War I and considerable losses to its fleet, strategizing at Cunard's Liverpool headquarters became more conservative. Ideas of building big, fast liners were pushed aside, at least for the next ten years or so. Among other reasons, it was widely believed that the postwar Atlantic passenger trade would be more moderate. In fact, the immigrant trade would dwindle substantially following the installation of American immigration quotas of 1924. The old third-class and steerage quarters, for example, had to be refitted and restyled as a less spartan, very affordable tourist class. Among the new Cunarders of the early 1920s were the *Samaria* (**opposite, top**) and her two sisters, *Scythia* and *Laconia*. Weighing a moderate 20,000 tons and with a comparatively slow speed of 16 knots, she had modest interiors and a simple, single-stack exterior. [Built by Cammel, Laird & Company Limited, Birkenhead, England, 1921. 19,602 gross tons; 624 feet long; 73 feet wide. Steam turbines, twin screw. Service speed 16 knots. 2,190 passengers (350 first-class, 340 second-class, 1,500 third-class).]

AURANIA. Cunard built an even more moderate series of six sister ships (*Antonia, Andania, Ausonia, Aurania* (**opposite, bottom**), *Alaunia,* and *Ascania*) primarily for their alternate Canadian services to Quebec City and Montreal, or to Halifax in the winter when the ice-clogged St. Lawrence was closed. In many ways, these ships were offshoots of the larger, grander *Aquitania*. [Built by Swan, Hunter & Wigham Richardson Shipbuilders Limited, Newcastle, England, 1924. 13,984 gross tons; 538 feet long; 65 feet wide. Steam turbines, twin screw. Service speed 15 knots. 1,688 passengers (510 cabin-class, 1,178 third-class).]

LANCASTRIA. Seen here off Liverpool on November 7, 1938 (**above**), the *Lancastria* belonged to the Glasgow-based Anchor Line and was initially named *Tyrrhenia*. She was bought by Cunard before completion, and retained her original name for almost two years before it changed to *Lancastria* during a winter refit in 1924. She had no identical or even similar sisters within the Cunard fleet, but nevertheless was a popular Atlantic liner as well as one-class cruise ship. She sailed from New York, Southampton, and Liverpool in the 1930s. [Built by William Beardmore & Company, Glasgow, Scotland, 1922. 16,243 gross tons; 578 feet long; 70 feet wide; 30-foot draft. Steam turbines, twin screw. Service speed 16.5 knots. 1,846 passengers (235 first-class, 355 second-class, 1,256 third-class).]

CARINTHIA. A new breed of single-stack Cunarders was designed with fancier quarters, better fittings, and more artistic detailing when they were completed in 1925. Two were named *Carinthia* (**above**) and *Franconia*. Cunard directors saw increasing potential in a business apart from the North Atlantic route: long-term, luxurious cruises. Earlier, in 1922, the *Laconia* had been chartered for a four-month cruise around the world. It was, in fact, the first such voyage in ocean liner history and was a great success, with similar trips soon following. Cunard directed both the *Carinthia* and *Franconia* to make as many as three such trips a year: two that departed New York in winter (but on different itineraries), and one in fall. They lasted as long as 160 days, touching at over thirty-five ports and were priced, by 1930, from $900, including all shore excursions. In many ways, Cunard set the benchmark for luxury cruising in the 1920s and 1930s. (Built by Vickers Armstrong Shipbuilders Limited, Barrow-in-Furness, England, 1925. 20,227 gross tons; 624 feet long; 73 feet wide. Steam turbines, twin screw. Service speed 16.5 knots. 1,650 passengers (240 first-class, 460 second-class, 950 third-class).]

MAJESTIC. By the early 1930s, the White Star Line was ailing. Cunard's determined rival had never quite recovered from the *Titanic* tragedy in 1912, and began to fall on hard times following the Wall Street Crash. As its potential bankruptcy would surely taint the national image, the British government agreed to loan Cunard additional monies to complete the *Queen Mary* and build a companion liner if Cunard would merge with—and therefore save—White Star Line. Thus, in July 1934, the corporate identity changed to Cunard–White Star Limited. Cunard inherited White Star's fleet, including some of the largest liners then afloat. The *Majestic*, for example, seen here entering the King George V Graving Dock at Southampton on February 3, 1935 (**opposite, top**), was considered the largest ship prior to the debut of the French *Normandie* that summer. But having been built back in 1914 (as the *Bismarck* for the Hamburg America Line), she was an aging, less competitive ship by the mid-1930s. Burdened by structural problems, she soon became one of the

first on Cunard's disposal list of 1935–36. After all, the sparkling new *Queen Mary* was due in May 1936 and old liners such as the *Majestic* were fading to obsolescence. The former White Star flagship was sold to Scottish scrappers for $400,000, but was then resold to the British Admiralty. Renamed the HMS *Caledonia*, she found use as a permanently moored cadet training ship for 1,500 boys and 500 junior officers at Rosyth. Just as the war started in September 1939, she caught fire, burned out, and sank at her anchorage. Her remains were scrapped gradually, with the job ending in 1943. [Built by Blohm & Voss Shipbuilders, Hamburg, Germany, 1914–22. 56,551 gross tons; 950 feet long; 100 feet wide. Steam turbines, quadruple screw. Service speed 23.5 knots. 2,145 passengers (750 first-class, 545 second-class, 850 third-class).]

OLYMPIC. Another great liner inherited by Cunard during White Star merger was the *Olympic* (**opposite, bottom**), sister ship to the ill-fated *Titanic*. She had survived World War I and resumed commercial sailings, but soon struggled with fewer passengers in the early 1930s. In her adventurous history, she rammed a warship in 1911, collided with another passenger ship in New York harbor in 1924, and later, in thick fog, rammed and sank the famed Nantucket Lightship. Eight of the lightship's crew perished and Cunard–White Star subsequently paid out a staggering $500,000 in compensation claims. She is seen in this view, dated May 16, 1934, arriving at New York just after the tragic collision and with her flag at half-mast. Soon afterward, she, too, joined Cunard's disposal list. Rumored to be sold to Mussolini's government for use as a troop transport for his East African campaigns, she was sold instead to British shipbreakers for some $350,000. The demolition was divided in halves: the upper deck and parts of the hull were demolished at Jarrow, and the remains were towed to Inverkeithing in Scotland for the last rites. [Built by Harland & Wolff Limited, Belfast, Northern Ireland, 1911. 45,324 gross tons; 882 feet long; 92 feet wide. Steam triple-expansion engines, triple screw. Service speed 21 knots. 2,764 passengers as built (1,054 first-class, 510 second-class, 1,200 third-class).]

BERENGARIA. In compensation for the wartime loss of the giant *Lusitania* in 1915, Cunard was awarded the former Hamburg America liner *Imperator*. First completed in 1913, she was the largest ship then afloat. Laid up at Hamburg throughout the First World War, she was taken by the Americans as reparations after the armistice in 1919, and was placed in service as the trooper USS *Imperator*. Passed to the British government and then to Cunard, she sailed again under her original German name in 1919–20. Afterward, she was taken in for thorough refitting and upgrading, then returned to Atlantic service as the rechristened *Berengaria*. A very popular ship in the 1920s, she, too, was forced into cheap "booze cruising" in the Depression and was even nicknamed "Bargain-area" by the less affluent souls that now strolled her decks and filled her lounges. She was, however, kept on as a running mate to the new *Queen Mary*, beginning in May 1936. The older ship was needed, at least until the *Queen Elizabeth* was due in the winter of 1940. But the end for the *Berengaria* came sooner than Cunard managers had planned. She began to suffer from fires, often from aged wiring, and eventually lost her U. S. Coast Guard sailing certificate. It was all quite embarrassing for Cunard and, quietly and without passengers, she returned to Southampton for

the last time in March 1938. She was soon sold to scrappers, but not completely broken-up until after World War II ended in 1946. In this dramatic view in March 1937 (*above*), the *Berengaria* is seen in one of the greatest collections of prewar luxury liners at New York. The *Europa* of the North German Lloyd is at the top, berthed at Pier 86; next is the Italian Line's *Rex* sharing Pier 88 with the *Normandie* of the French Line; and finally at Cunard–White Star's Pier 90, the *Georgic*, a 1932-built liner (in fact the last for the White Star Line), is just across from the *Berengaria*. Three of these liners, the *Europa*, *Rex*, and *Normandie*, were Blue Riband holders, predecessors to the *Queen Mary*'s firm and final record of August 1938. [Built by Bremer Vulkan Shipyards, Hamburg, Germany, 1913. 52,226 gross tons; 919 feet long; 98 feet wide. Steam turbines, quadruple screw. Service speed 23 knots. 2,723 passengers in 1921 (972 first-class, 630 second-class, 606 third-class, 515 tourist-class).]

The *Berengaria*'s German heritage was quite visible in her first-class smoking room (*opposite, top*), which resembled a Bavarian hunting lodge. Her first-class dining room (*opposite, bottom*) followed the decor of other Atlantic express liners of the time.

MAURETANIA. After the *Queen Mary* entered service in May 1936, a new age seemed to begin. The older liners, those four-stacked Edwardian "floating palaces," seemed to disappear rather quickly. With the exception of the *Aquitania*, which was expected to go for scrap in 1940, other Cunard–White Star giants such as the *Olympic*, *Majestic*, and *Berengaria* went off to the breakers. Oldest of all, the beloved *Mauretania* made her final crossing in September 1934, just as the *Mary* was being launched up in Scotland. There was a tearful but spirited auction of the old Cunarder's fittings before she steamed off for Rosyth and the junkyard. In this sad scene (*above*), dated July 30, 1935, the *Mauretania*, by then called the "Old Lady of the Seas," has already lost all of her starboard lifeboats and their davits. The faded, rusting funnels are next to go. In the foreground are the last remains of the former German warship *Bayern*.

Chapter II

ROYAL DEBUT

The 1930s was indeed the high-water mark for the great Atlantic ocean liners: the ultimate era in luxury, size, splendor, and even in fantasy. This period produced the most wondrous of these ships. There was Germany's *Bremen* and *Europa,* and a pair from Mussolini's Italy, the *Rex* and the *Conte di Savoia.* But it was the French and then the British that produced liners especially created to pull out all stops and take all records. The exquisite French *Normandie* was commissioned in the spring of 1935; Britain's splendid *Queen Mary* a year later. Their creators had three lofty goals: to build liners that would not only exceed 1,000 feet in length, but also tip the scales well over 75,000 tons; to make them the fastest ships on the Atlantic Ocean; and to create dazzling national ambassadors of design, decor, and technology.

But there were the expected differences. While the *Normandie* was sleek and modern, rakish and even very racy, the *Queen Mary* was stately and more graceful—a grand throwback to the great ocean liners that preceded her. Though the *Normandie* was 1,028 feet in length and therefore distinctively the longest liner afloat, the *Mary* had the slightly greater tonnage and was therefore listed

as the largest ship. While the *Normandie* was indeed very powerful and was the Blue Riband champion in her maiden year, the *Queen Mary* proved even faster and took the prized Riband from her Gallic rival. And while the French flagship impressed many with her exceptional, glamorous style, it was the new Cunarder that won the hearts of even more voyagers with her cozier, perhaps less pretentious decor and tone. Like so many superliners before them, the *Normandie* and the *Queen Mary* were great competitors, gloriously seeking greater shares of the fabled transatlantic trade.

The *Queen Mary* remained the *Normandie's* greatest rival. But Cunard promised to be the more successful: the company was planning the first two-ship express team on the Atlantic, with weekly service in each direction for most of the year. As the *Queen Mary* firmly and finally took the Blue Riband from the *Normandie* in August 1938, the second of the Cunard's giants—a ship bigger still—was being prepared for launching at Clydeside in Scotland. She would be royally baptized as the *Queen Elizabeth.* The pair would run as a team, it was planned, beginning in April 1940.

QUEEN MARY. Cunard became interested in a possible superliner in the mid-1920s, but for delivery in the early 1930s (presumably to replace the likes of the aging *Mauretania* of 1907). Between 1926 and 1928, planners diligently began examining every aspect of contemporary marine engineering, design, and decoration. Above all else, Cunard was seeking the distinct advantage of offering the first-ever twin-liner Atlantic express service, with one ship leaving each terminal port on a weekly rotation. Even the skilled Germans, with their new *Bremen* and *Europa* (completed in 1929 and 1930, respectively), could not match this prized offering. Their ships were not fast enough, and thus needed a third ship, the *Columbus*, to maintain weekly sailings in each direction. It was hardly an improvement compared to, say, Cunard's existing trio—the *Mauretania, Aquitania,* and *Berengaria.*

The design of a big, new Cunard express liner also had to meet other requirements: prompt port turnarounds, sailings for eleven months of the year without major repairs, substantial reserve power, strong construction to withstand the rigors of the North Atlantic, and a consistent operating speed between 27.6 and 28.9 knots. Such a new ship would, it was estimated, consume upwards of 11,000 tons of fuel per crossing, compared to the 3,800 tons for the veteran *Mauretania* or the 5,000 tons for the larger *Berengaria.* Studies were made for the choice in propulsion machinery (alone, fourteen different systems were examined including a latter-day use of coal). While steam turbine drive was eventually selected, even the trendy turbo-electric type was considered (a system that the French used for their giant, the *Normandie*).

The building order for the new ship was sensibly given to John Brown & Company at Clydebank, in May 1930 (*opposite*). They had built the *Lusitania* and the *Aquitania,* the latter of which strongly influenced the new giant in both design and style. Even as work began on the Cunarder, John Brown was finishing the 42,000-ton *Empress of Britain,* the stunning new flagship for Canadian Pacific. [Built by John Brown & Company Limited, Clydebank, Scotland, 1930–36. 81,235 gross tons; 1,018 feet long; 118 feet wide; 39-foot draft. Steam turbines, quadruple screw. Service speed 28.5 knots. 2,139 passengers as built (776 first-class, 784 tourist-class, 579 third-class).]

For the new Cunarder (*above*), there were tests, experiments, missions aboard Cunarders and other liners, mountains of paperwork, statistical studies, special examinations of such liners as the *Aquitania, Bremen,* and *Ile de France,* and even the construction of a large test sewerage system on the roof of the Cunard Building at Liverpool that used specially devised glass tubes and colored liquids. Every aspect had to be considered: crew members, engine spaces, kitchen design, bedrooms, public areas, storage, cargo handling, baggage, offices, hospital space, and even closets for several hundred vacuum cleaners. Expected to exceed 75,000 tons, but possibly closer to 80,000, the new ship was unlike anything in existence. Her needs and demands were extremely special. Every department at Cunard worked in close cooperation, often well into the night behind lighted windows of the Liverpool headquarters. Saturdays and even Sundays meant little; phone calls at 2 and 3 A.M. became normal.

Then, in December 1931, a year into the project, Cunard suddenly and abruptly halted construction. Due to the crippling effects of the Depression, Cunard was about to realize a severe trading loss of nearly $10 million for 1931. Overall, British earnings from passenger shipping on the Atlantic had dropped from $45 million in 1928 to just under $20 million by 1931. First-class trade, for example, fell from 175,000 passengers in 1926 to 116,000 in 1931. Cunard was seriously and rightfully worried. The most pressing problem was the new Cunarder. Should the project be stopped? Should she be sold? If so, to whom? At worst, should the existing steel structure be scrapped? The grand project had already cost Cunard nearly $6 million.

Once construction was officially halted, over 3,000 shipyard workers were fired in 1931, an untimely two weeks before Christmas. Another 10,000 workers from subsidiary companies were also dismissed. Only a bare staff of 440 remained at the John Brown yard, mostly draftsmen, senior craftworkers, and deputies.

The large steel frame of the liner sat like a naked skeleton for twenty-eight months: silent and rusting, a haven to birds and their nests (*opposite*). In desperation, Cunard was reported to have inquired if the French Line was willing to abandon their super-liner project (the *Normandie*), hoping that if it was so, Cunard would do the same. The Liverpool head office promptly denied this story. In reality, Cunard could not abandon their new express liner. While shipyard work was halted, the company was merely awaiting extra financing. All of Cunard's other express ships had to be replaced. The silent new liner was technically the smallest ship—even at over 1,000 feet in length and as much as 80,000 tons—which could fulfill the conditions and obligations of a twin-liner express service with "floating hotel" standards. She would be an evolutionary vessel, with very powerful engines, that would feature high standard, contemporary accommodations.

Fortunately, the British government came to the rescue by the spring of 1934, but with provisions. In return for guaranteed loans, Cunard would have to merge with its former rival, the financially troubled White Star Line. To this, Cunard was quick to agree. Cunard–White Star Limited was promptly created, with the Cunard company getting 62 percent of the stock. In return, the government provided a three-prong loan: approximately $15 million to complete the new liner, $25 million for a future sister or running mate, and about $6 million for emergency working capital. At Yard #534, work on the ship resumed on April 3, 1934. One of the first tasks was to remove 130 tons of accumulated rust on the steel frames.

One of the more charming stories in ocean liner history is the tale concerning the choice of a name for the new Cunarder (*above*). As the ship neared completion, the company was over-whelmed with suggestions—everything from "Britannia" and "Galicia," to "Hamptonia" and "Clydania." There were, rather expectedly, some royalist proposals: "Princess Elizabeth," "Princess Margaret Rose," and even "Marina," for the popular Princess Marina, then recently married to the Duke of Kent, son of King George V and Queen Mary. The most persistent story is, however, that Cunard directors preferred "Victoria." But when George V was asked for his royal approval, he supposedly misun-derstood and, in hearing the description, "England's greatest queen," thought only of his wife. No matter, "Queen Mary" seemed an ideal choice, as the government had wanted some-thing nationalistic and unifying. In fact, 1935 was George and Mary's Silver Jubilee year, and the popular royal couple was largely seen as standing icons in an otherwise rapidly changing Britain. In actuality, Queen Mary, still wearing her Victorian dresses, choker pearls, and toque hats, was delighted with the honor of the new ship bearing her name. It was a tightly kept secret, however, until the formal launching in September 1934.

The King and Queen, together with the Prince of Wales (later Edward VIII, the Duke of Windsor) arrived by train at Clydebank from their summer retreat at Balmoral on September 26, 1934, for the formal launching of the new Cunarder. It was the first time that a reigning British queen was to name a merchant ship. In due course, her daughter-in-law (Queen Elizabeth The Queen Mother) and her granddaughter (Queen Elizabeth II) would do the same. From behind a glass shield, at just after three in the afternoon, Her Majesty—looking out onto a sea of 200,000 umbrellas huddled under the rain—swung a bottle of Australian wine into the towering bow. In her first public speech as Queen Consort, she announced the name of the vessel. "I am happy to name this ship *Queen Mary*. I wish success to her and all who sail in her." A hush passed through the otherwise silent crowd. The

secrecy of the grand ship's name had ended. Loud cheers went up. This view of Queen Mary dates from just after the Second World War, in 1947 (*opposite, top*).

Thousands more spectators watched the launch from the opposite shore of the Clyde (*opposite, bottom*), as still others observed from tugboats, specially chartered pleasure craft, and from the decks of the Anchor liner *Tuscania*, which was turned into a floating grandstand. Within forty-five seconds, the 30,000-ton shell was waterborne. Life for "the *Mary*," as she would be affectionately known, had begun (*above, left*). With pride, George V called it "the stateliest ship in being."

Following her launching, the *Queen Mary* was moved to the fitting-out berth at the John Brown yard (*above, right*).

Armies of workmen were busy around the clock, as seen in this nighttime photo dated March 6, 1936 (*above*), to ensure that the *Queen Mary* would be ready for her gala maiden voyage that May. Once fitted-out, she was also ready for those first appraisals.

Despite several splashes of modern art in the public lounges, the new liner was quite conservative, in the tradition of a fine hotel. Overall, she was a warm and comfortable ship, with less of the massive and grander tones of the *Normandie*. She lacked the innovative glitter and the almost pretentious extravagance of her French rival. Instead, the *Mary* followed in the established spirit and style of earlier Cunarders, namely the *Aquitania* of 1914. There were soft sofas and upholstered armchairs, pylon lamps and fireplaces, glossy veneers, chrome and glass fixtures, carpets of florals and swirls, brass handrails and wood-framed clocks, murals and thick velvet drapes, and a marble medallion depicting Queen

Mary. In this photo (*opposite, top*), dated March 6, 1936, the first-class dining room is being readied for her first public inspection. Above all else, the *Queen Mary* was unmistakably a British ship, assuredly a Cunarder.

The first-class library, seen here in a view dating from May 27, 1936 (*opposite, bottom*), was fully stocked by the time of her maiden voyage.

In April 1936, the *Mary* superbly carried out her speed trials up and down the Irish Sea, reaching a high speed of 32.84 knots. Other reports suggested that she "well exceeded 33 knots." In comparison, these figures made a favorable showing against the *Mauretania*'s best run of 27.22 knots, the *Bremen*'s 28.51, and even the *Normandie*'s recent record of 29.98. Indeed, the *Queen Mary* would try for the Blue Riband.

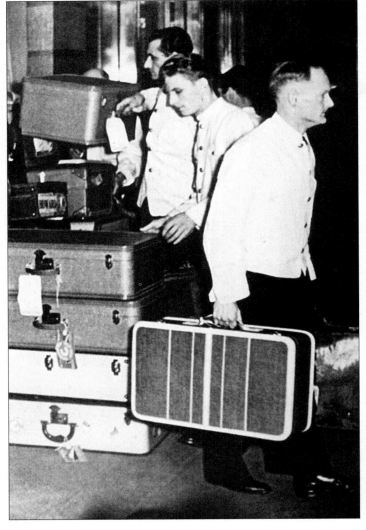

No less than eighteen special trains carried thousands of spectators to the Southampton Docks on May 27 to see her off on her maiden voyage to New York (seen here at Clydesbank, *opposite, top*). Other ships, tugs, and excursion craft filled the Solent, forming an enormous flotilla. Scores of journalists and photographers were on hand, later sending their prized efforts by train and auto to anxious Fleet Street editors. One clever London photographer outpaced them all, however. His films were delivered by carrier pigeons from the Southampton countryside.

Thousands of visitors came to Southampton in May 1936 just to see the *Queen Mary*, already the most publicized and well-known liner in the world. Queen Mary herself, accompanied by many members of the royal family, toured the liner at the Ocean Dock. Victorian in her tastes and not at all keen on the then-popular Art Deco style, Her Majesty commented in her diary that evening, "Today, I toured the new *Queen Mary*. Not as bad on the inside as I had expected!" In this photo (*opposite, bottom*), armies of stewards sort and then deliver the mountains of luggage that went aboard the *Queen Mary* for her maiden voyage to New York, which departed from Southampton on May 27.

Seen here (*above*) on June 1, 1936, waiting at anchor in New York's Lower Bay before proceeding to her West 50th Street berth, the *Queen Mary*'s crossing was filled with gaiety, exuberance, and certainly celebration, but there had been some tense moments. Engine problems developed in the English Channel soon after the liner's call at Cherbourg. Pieces of turbine blades, assumed to have accidentally broken off, were missing and one essential blade was actually fractured. The captain, his immediate officers, the Cunard chairman, and onboard representatives from John Brown were concerned throughout the voyage, as the severity of the problem could not be fully determined until the liner reached New York. But what if the press got wind of the situation or, far worse, what if the new *Queen* broke down on her maiden voyage?

There was widespread talk, of course, that the *Mary* would take the Blue Riband from the *Normandie*. Although she reached 30.64 knots on at least one day, there was considerable fog off the Grand Banks of Newfoundland—a problem for the shipping industry for decades—which reduced the liner's speed. In that region, though hardly noticed by her joyous passengers, a wreath was dropped overboard in the vicinity where the *Titanic* took her final plunge twenty-four years earlier.

When the *Queen Mary* (**right**), finally reached the specially—albeit hurriedly—built Pier 90, the *New York Times* reported, "A gentle blizzard of torn paper appeared in the great canyons between the buildings, bursting on the hot summerlike air as suddenly and as decoratively as a flight of pigeons." Once docked, a steady round of welcoming banquets, ceremonial exchanges, luncheons, toasts, press tours, and visits by tens of thousands of New Yorkers began. Souvenir hunters were at a brisk pace. One woman reportedly even tried to undo one of the paintings in the main lounge.

Her noted qualities of gentle comfort and overall warmth may well be an important reason why the *Queen Mary* became the only financially successful superliner of the late 1930s, earning a profit from the very start. In 1937, her first full year of service, she was rated as the most popular liner on the Atlantic. Along with the residual effects of the Depression, lingering resentment from World War I and growing anti-Nazi sentiment reduced non-national passenger lists on German ships like the *Bremen* and *Europa*. Italy's *Rex* and *Conte di Savoia* suffered as well, primarily because their Southern Mediterranean routing was not as desirable as the northern route which stopped at very popular Channel ports. Finally, the *Normandie*, absolutely the most decoratively stunning liner ever to sail the Atlantic, the most advanced in overall design, and the most serious rival to the new Cunard flagship, intimidated many "ordinary passengers" by her extreme luxury. Quite possibly, her opulent tone was over-sold by French Line publicists. Apart from the *Queen Mary*, it would seem that the only very successful new liner in the otherwise hard-pressed 1930s was the 36,000-ton Dutch *Nieuw Amsterdam*. Commissioned in May 1938, she was, however, not in the actual superliner class.

In these views, we see several of the *Mary*'s public areas: a section of the cabin-class dining room (**above, left**), a bar in tourist class (**above, right**), the plush Veranda Grill Restaurant (**opposite, top**), the cabin-class writing room (**opposite, middle**), and, one of her finest amenities, the splendid indoor swimming pool (**opposite, bottom**). Let it be stated, however, that not all Britons reached for pen in praise of the new Cunarder, the nation's finest maritime flag-waver. To some, her innards often resembled an Art Deco-style, Leicester Square cinema; to others, she was simply "too Teddy-bear." One critic went so far as to label her first-class public rooms in particular as "Woolworth five-and-dime." One passenger later complained that some of her lounges had all the warmth of a political office in Warsaw.

Seen here (**above**) in the King George V Graving Dock at Southampton during her first winter overhaul, the *Mary* was a ship of seemingly endless statistics. She had, as examples, four million rivets, 600 clocks, and fifty-six different kinds of woods used in her interiors. On her maiden voyage, with 1,849 passengers aboard (290 less than absolute capacity), she was stocked with such items as 14,000 bottles of wine, 50,000 eggs, 17,000 lbs. of fresh fish, 20,000 bottles of milk, and 25,000 packets of cigarettes. In the two forward holds, she carried 3,500 bags of mail.

The *Queen Mary* finally captured the Blue Riband after nearly three months, in August 1936. She had crossed the Atlantic, between Ambrose Light and Bishop Rock, in just three minutes under four days, with an average speed of 30.68 knots. This surpassed the *Normandie*'s latest record of four days and three hours, at an average of 30.31 knots. Cunard was, however, quite casual about their latest achievement, even declining the Riband's Hales Trophy and a special welcome at Southampton (though there was a grand reception just the same). A company spokesman simply described the record-breaking crossing as "all in a day's work for us." Content with his efforts, the ship's chief engineer added, "I think we should all be surprised if we really opened her out!" From a yachting cruise in the Mediterranean, Edward VIII wired: "Sincere congratulations on the *Queen Mary*'s fine record."

Unbeknownst to most, that August voyage had also been a highly secret, very calculated test crossing. It was not only a gauge of the *Mary*'s highest capabilities, but also gathered important information for the design of her intended running mate, that second Cunard giant that was to begin construction on the Clyde in December 1936.

The *Normandie* recaptured the Blue Riband in March 1937, with an average of 30.9 knots. The French flagship even improved on her own record, in the following August, with an average of 31.2 knots. However, the Cunarder finally and firmly took the title of "world's fastest" in August 1938, with an average of 31.6 knots, a crossing of three days and twenty hours. The *Mary* retained the Riband for fourteen years until, in July 1952, it passed to America's technologically brilliant, enormously powerful *United States*.

QUEEN ELIZABETH. Cunard first publicly announced the decision to build a running mate to the *Queen Mary* in February 1936, just three months before the *Mary*'s maiden sailing to New York. It would seem to be an after-thought or a last-minute decision, because Cunard—always cautious and even secretive—had waited to the very last possible moment before going public. A running mate, the second in a pair of express liners, was always part of the overall plan, even at the peak of the disheartening Depression, when so many ideas and plans were shelved. There would be little value, of course, in running a five-day express service with just one ship.

The *Queen Mary* had been a groundbreaker in both ocean-liner design and construction. She was, after all, the first 1,000-footer, the first to exceed 80,000 tons, and—perhaps more importantly—the first for that projected fast service with five-day crossings. There was considerable experimentation with this three-stacker. Alternately, the second Cunard giant was a successor in ways to a new generation of super ships: namely the *Bremen*, *Europa*, *Rex*, and *Conte di Savoia*, certainly the *Normandie* and, of course, the *Mary* herself. Most of the groundwork had been laid, and so all Cunard had to do was rework and improve upon the *Mary*'s design. The earlier ship's twenty-eight boilers, for example, were reduced to twelve in the new liner. Further developments included less-cluttered upper decks, two funnels instead of three, no well deck forward, and the bow on the second liner would have a sharper rake. There were, of course, other changes in the second giant (under construction at John Brown's on the Clyde, **opposite**): a bow anchor, an added twelve feet in length, about 2,000 tons greater tonnage and over 250 additional passenger berths. [Built by John Brown & Company Limited, Clydebank, Scotland, 1936–40. 83,673 gross tons; 1,031 feet long; 118 feet wide; 39-foot draft. Steam turbines, quadruple screw. Service speed 28.5 knots. 2,283 passengers (823 first-class, 662 cabin-class, 798 tourist-class).]

The new Cunarder was nameless for a time, even after construction started in December 1936, (*above*). Rumor was that she would be called "King George V," honoring the beloved late monarch and husband of Queen Mary who had died the previous January. Though the rumors that the two liners would become "the King and Queen of the Atlantic" proved wrong, the ships did, however, become the "Queens of the Atlantic." In February 1938, Cunard revealed that *Queen Elizabeth* was the choice, honoring the widely popular former Duchess of York, who became Queen Consort (and later Queen Elizabeth The Queen Mother) when her husband ascended the throne as George VI in December 1936.

Just as for the *Queen Mary* in September 1934, huge crowds were at the John Brown yard for the launching exactly four years later, on September 27, 1938, for the naming and launch of the *Elizabeth*. Fittingly, Queen Elizabeth did the honors (*below*), accompanied by Princess Elizabeth and Princess Margaret. This time, however, the occasion had an added dimension. Radio microphones were hidden in the slipway so all of Britain, as well as its territories overseas, could hear the roar and rumble as the huge hull went down the ways and safely into the Clyde. Even dowager Queen Mary was listening back home in London.

Soon after her royal launching, the *Elizabeth* was moved to John Brown's fitting-out berth, seen in this atmospheric photo (**top**) being led by the tug *Flying Eagle*, with the shipyard's special heavy-lift crane in the background. A year later, in September of 1939, both King George VI and Queen Elizabeth planned to visit the new superliner as construction progressed (**left**). She was scheduled to begin her first sailing to New York, a partner to the *Queen Mary*, on April 24, 1940. Cunard's long-awaited dream, the world's first and finest twin liner express service, would then be realized. However, war was declared on September 3, and the royal visit was canceled. The King and Queen were forced to remain in London while work on the big liner suddenly went silent. Work crews at John Brown were ordered by the Admiralty to turn their full attention to far more urgent warship construction and repair. The new *Queen Elizabeth* was a merchant ship and therefore considered less important—or so the British government ministers thought.

Chapter III

THE QUEENS AT WAR

During World War II, for almost seven long, arduous years (1939–1946), the Queens were heroic troopships for the Allied cause . . . the elusive "Grey Ghosts." In all, they carried over two million Allied personnel across to Britain for the eventual invasion of Normandy and the subsequent liberation of Europe. With their peacetime fineries either removed or not yet in place, and their exteriors painted over entirely in disguising grays, the *Queen Mary* and *Queen Elizabeth* sailed in top secrecy, invisible at night and pushed to urgent speeds. No warships could escort them nor Nazi U-boats catch them, and they averaged 15,000 soldier-passengers per trip. In fact, the *Queen Mary*, on a July 1943 passage out of New York, carried 16,683 souls at one time, a record still unsurpassed. Comparatively, in peacetime comfort and luxury, she could take up to 2,100 passengers. According to Britain's Prime Minister Winston Churchill, "By continuously delivering Allied invasion forces, the two Queens helped to lessen the war in Europe by at least a year."

Peter Chase, an Englishman sent to Canada for special military training early in the war, returned home on the 83,600-ton *Queen Elizabeth* in November 1942. "We boarded by tenders off Prince Edward Island on the ship's troop run from New York to Gourock in Scotland," he remembered. "It was a five-day passage. She zig-zagged all the way, making 30 knots and sometimes more. She was so fast that we sometimes thought she might turn on her side. We called her 'the great boat in gray.' Of course, there were no military escorts or convoys for a ship like the 'Liz.' Certainly, the U-boats could not catch us."

"There were two meals a day: six in the morning for breakfast and six in the evening for dinner," added Chase. "There was no lunch during the war onboard either the 'Lizzie' or the *Mary*, names we also used. There was plenty of food onboard, all of it supplied in America, but to a ration-strapped Englishman, there seemed to be 'oceans' of butter and bread. She was still not completely fitted out as a trooper, however. I was assigned to a former two-bedded stateroom, but that was refitted with seventeen bunks. They were four high and about four inches from the bottom and three inches from the ceiling. There was a six-inch gun at the stern and it was used for daily target practice. Douglas Fairbanks, Jr. was aboard, as was Edward G. Robinson, who gave a concert to entertain the troops and who later signed several thousand autographs. We had over 13,000 aboard our crossing, plus over 1,000 crew."

Scraped, cleaned, and polished, the *Queen Elizabeth* entered luxury service in the fall of 1946, with the *Mary* reappearing the following summer. Routed on five-day crossings between New York, Cherbourg, and Southampton, first-class fares began at $350. They were among the very first luxury ships to resume commercial sailing, and reservations were expectedly in great demand. "I had a businessman as a client, a rich diamond merchant, who traveled only in suites before the war," recalled Robert Bloch, a New York City travel agent. "But in November 1946, on the *Elizabeth*'s return peacetime maiden crossing from New York, he settled for an upper bunk in a quad in cabin class."

When the *Queen Mary* reached New York on September 1, 1939, with a record 2,139 worried passengers aboard, the political situation in Europe was extremely tense. Cunard decided that, in view of the uncertainty, all further sailings would be canceled and the ship laid-up on the south side of Pier 90. She was supposedly merely waiting for the end of what was called "the brief political crisis" abroad. In fact, the end was nearly six years away. The Cunarder was quickly repainted in gray (a small section of the stern area is still in commercial colors in this view, ***above***). A cloak of mystery surrounded the *Queen Mary* and many other liners lying in New York. On September 15, in an unusual and completely unannounced move, the *Mary* was moved by harbor tugs from the north side of Pier 90 to the south slip. The *Normandie*, so the French Line felt, was also more secure in the safe waters of New York harbor. She is visible just across the slip at Pier 88.

With the two great bows of the *Normandie* and *Queen Mary* in formation on Manhattan's West Side (***opposite, top***), the Cunarder waited for her next orders. She was, of course, supposed to return to Cherbourg and Southampton according to the posted schedules. But the risk of crossing the North Atlantic was already too great. Some 700 security guards were posted to the Cunard flagship, and many of her crew were sent home on smaller, less important Cunard Line ships. Rumors about her future circulated quickly: would she go off to war, would she be converted to an armed transport, or, prompted by a suggestion from a misguided Member of Parliament, would she be sold to the still-neutral Americans? There were at least two CIA reports that Nazi agents in New York planned to blow up the ship. Once, during a safety drill at Pier 90, one of lowered lifeboats quickly flooded. It had been deliberately punctured with holes. By night, searchlights played on the *Mary*, giving her an almost sinister, prisonlike atmosphere.

In Britain, rumors circulated that Nazi agents planned to sabo-

tage or even bomb the brand new *Queen Elizabeth*. In February 1940, a deliberate rumor was set by the British government that the *Elizabeth* would be soon leaving the Clyde and, via the Irish Sea, headed for Southampton and dry-docking prior to delivery. Luftwaffe bombers were waiting in the channel. But instead, once clear of the Clyde, the gray-painted, incomplete *Elizabeth* never turned to port and instead sped to sea, clearing the top of Northern Ireland. While said to be headed for the safety of Halifax, she was actually routed to New York and the far more secure berthing of Cunard's Pier 90. In this U. S. Coast Guard aerial view (***opposite, bottom***), we see the liner approaching New York. Her intended maiden voyage, in peacetime livery and dressed in flags, would have to wait. On the afternoon of March 7, the mighty *Elizabeth*, with a reduced escort of welcoming tugs, sailed past the Battery and up the lower Hudson River (***above***). Whistles from every craft sounded in a welcoming salute. Because of her heroic flight from wartime Britain, she was dubbed the "Grey Ghost."

For two weeks, beginning on March 7, 1940, the three largest ocean liners of their time—the *Normandie* (left), the *Queen Mary* (center), and, biggest of all, the brand new *Queen Elizabeth*—were berthed together between West 48th and West 50th streets (**above**). New York dockers quickly dubbed them the "Monsters."

The *Mary* quietly departed for a long, highly secretive voyage to Australia via Brazil, the South African Cape, and across the Indian Ocean in April 1940. She is seen here (**opposite, top**) in her final days at New York's Pier 90, with the *Normandie* at the top, the *Mary* and *Elizabeth* just below, and the *Vulcania* at Pier 92, a ship then still making commercial sailings to and from Mussolini's Italy.

The *Elizabeth* sailed off on a somber afternoon, with the aft end of the laid-up *Normandie* on the left (**opposite, middle**). Following in the *Mary*'s wake, she began the long, exhausting voyage to Australia in November 1940 (**opposite, bottom**). She was now, too, officially at war.

In 1940–41, both Queens operated across the Indian Ocean to Port Suez in Egypt, with stops en route at Trincomalee on Ceylon. They mostly ferried Australian troops (**above**) to reinforce the struggling North African campaigns, and returned with the wounded, evacuees, and even prisoners of war.

The *Queen Mary* returned to the Atlantic in May 1942, almost three years since her last appearance on those northern waters. In an ironic echo of her intended transatlantic luxury express service, she was put to work as a military shuttle between New York and Gourock in Scotland (**right**).

The *Mary*—and, beginning in December 1942, the *Queen Elizabeth* (*above*)—averaged 15,000 service personnel per crossing during World War II. In every respect, it was a staggering but well planned, efficient operation. She was, after all, carrying nearly eight times her intended capacity, plus her customary 1,100 crew.

The *Queen Mary* established the all-time record for any ship when, in July 1943, she departed from New York with 16,683 troops, passengers, and crew onboard (*left*). To this day, this remains the greatest number of souls ever to sail in one ship on a single voyage.

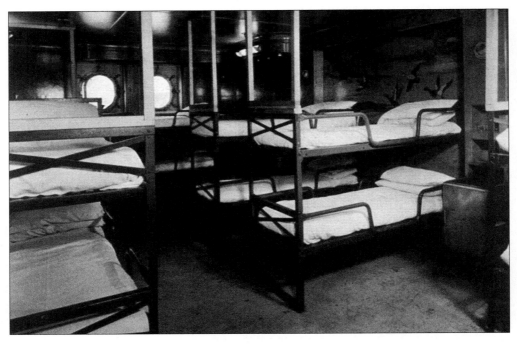

During the war, only the dining rooms were left partly intact onboard the two Queens. All other public areas were converted for the three daily shifts of sleeping during the war (*opposite, top*). Two-bedded first-class cabins, having been stripped of their finery, could accommodate up to eighteen, while suites could sleep as many as twenty-four.

In wartime, until as late as the spring of 1945, when victory in Europe was clearly in sight, the Queens operated under high security (*opposite, bottom*). Because of their great speeds, they were beyond the scope of any available escort craft. Even speedy destroyers were unable to keep up with them. Consequently, they sailed alone, blacked-out and usually steered on zigzag courses that were never followed twice.

Only one noted incident tarnished the otherwise exceptional record of the Queens in wartime. On October 2, 1942, while rounding the tip of Ireland at top speed, the *Queen Mary* (*above*) rammed, sliced in half, and sank the HMS *Curacoa*, a Royal Navy escort cruiser. The warship went down within three minutes, and all but twenty-six of her 364 crew members perished. Because of the danger of undetected Nazi U-boats, the *Mary*, with her 15,000 mostly soldier-passengers aboard, could not stop to rescue the survivors. She was forced, under strict orders, to continue on at top speed.

From the time of the Nazi surrender in May 1945 through the very end of that year, the Queens returned to New York to blazing welcomes: horns, sirens, waving flags, bed sheets from office windows, aircraft, Navy blimps overhead and, of course, spraying fire-boats. "A Job Well Done" read huge signs along the waterfront. In this view (*above*), dressed in flags, the *Queen Mary* arrives off Pier 90 on June 20, 1945 with 14,777 onboard. She was then considered to be the first official troopship with returning soldiers from the war in Europe. War in the Pacific would end a little more than a month later, in August.

In all, Cunard lost six ships to enemy action during World War II, and a further four were kept by the British Admiralty. Among the six was the *Lancastria*, which, during the evacuation of western France in June 1940, was bombed and sunk by Nazi aircraft. One of the most horrific casualties of that time, her losses were put at over 3,000. Other Cunarders gone by 1945 included the *Andania*, *Laconia*, and *Laurentic*. The celebrated cruise ship *Carinthia*, seen here (**below**) departing from Pier 54 on September 3, 1939 and already repainted in wartime grays, was also stricken from the company's fleet list. She was torpedoed off the Irish Coast by a Nazi submarine in June 1940.

With their safety assured following the German surrender in May 1945, the Queens returned to Southampton. They continued to carry troops, as well as the wounded, war brides and their babies, and even some passengers. Though the hulls and upper works remained gray, both ships had had their funnels repainted in peacetime Cunard colors in the summer of 1945 (as seen on the *Mary*, **opposite, top**). This alone was a symbol of the end of the war. The *Mary* was officially decommissioned from war duty thirteen months later, in September 1946 (seen **opposite, bottom**, passing the freshly restored *Elizabeth* at Southampton), and was sent back to her builder's yard for restoration and refitting. In July of the following year, she resumed commercial sailing between Southampton, Cherbourg, and New York. With the *Queen Elizabeth*, the two-ship team running weekly departures in

each direction was finally in place. It was the first of its kind in transatlantic ocean liner history, and created the most successful pair of liners of their time. For the next fifteen years or so, the *Queen Mary* and *Queen Elizabeth* were immensely profitable to Cunard and to Britain itself. Alone, they brought more tourists to bolster the British economy than any other passenger ships.

The classic, four-funneled *Aquitania*, which would have been scrapped in 1940, was retained by Cunard until 1950. She mostly ran an austerity service between Southampton and Halifax, carrying troops, refugees, immigrants, and the occasional tourists. At thirty-six years old, she was sent to the scrappers up in Scotland. In this scene (**above**), taken at Southampton's Ocean Dock on August 27, 1945, dock crews are clearing bomb damage to Berths 45 and 46, with the *Queen Mary* and the *Aquitania* in the background.

Chapter IV

GETTING THERE WAS HALF THE FUN

"Getting there was half the fun" surely ranks as one of the finest travel expressions ever. It says it all: the great adventure of a passage across the seas, as well as the fun, the rest, and the complete relaxation of a transatlantic voyage. The six words made it all seem wonderfully exciting and they belonged to Cunard, which was—in the ocean-travel-booming 1950s—the biggest, best known, and, in ways, the finest Atlantic shipping company. They were also at their peak. In 1957, Cunard had what they proudly called "the largest fleet on the Atlantic," with no less than a dozen passenger ships: from the giants *Queen Elizabeth* and *Queen Mary* to the *Mauretania*, *Caronia*, and *Britannic*, the combo ships *Media* and *Parthia*, the veteran *Scythia*, and four brand-new vessels—the sister ships *Saxonia*, *Ivernia*, *Carinthia*, and *Sylvania*. In the summertime peak, there might be as many as four sailings a week from New York to such ports as Cherbourg, Le Havre, Cobh, Southampton, and Liverpool.

The two Queens, crossing at over 28 knots, sailed almost every Wednesday from New York's Pier 90 and reached Cherbourg and Southampton late on the following Monday. On the weekend, the two giants crossed one another in the mid-Atlantic. The inbound ship arrived in New York on the following Tuesday, remaining overnight for replenishing and refueling before departing on Wednesday. For years, the ships were booked to capacity (and often over a year in advance) and earned millions, not only for Cunard, but for the British economy as well. It was a grand era, especially in first class on those huge Cunarders. "Those were days of chandeliers and palm court music, afternoon tea dances and fox furs," recalled Robin Davies, a Cunard steward beginning in 1950. "And, of course, there were personal servants, those big steamer trunks and even private automobiles in the hold. We had an endless procession of celebrities: Peter Sellers, Paul Newman, Elizabeth Taylor, Telly Savalas, Jim Backus, former President Eisenhower, the Duke and Duchess of Windsor, and even the Queen Mother. In 1954, she traveled over to New York and a rousing welcome on the *Elizabeth* and then, a month later, returned to Southampton on the *Mary*."

"There was very, very little intermingling between classes. Even the staff did not intermingle," remembered Tony Dent, who also sailed as a Cunard steward. "A first-class waiter on one of the Queens would never, ever be seen going ashore with, say, a tourist-class waiter. It was like "upstairs-downstairs," like those big English country houses we see on television and in films today. There were separations, codes, strict divisions. The Captain was feared and never spoken to, and passengers were never, ever addressed by name, but instead only as 'Sir' and 'Madame.'"

"The ships were three-class, of course, and there were definite differences," added Robin Davies. "In first class, there were two staff members to every passenger. The most preferable class, however, even by Cunard's suggestion, was cabin class. They called it the 'happy medium.' It was less stuffy, less rigid than first class, and yet not as informal as inexpensive tourist class, which was often used by students, budget tour groups, and immigrants. But by the 1960s, it all faded away. It was all gone, at least in the way we knew it, in all classes."

Bon voyage! Those two words once recollected fruit baskets delivered by impeccably uniformed stewards, staterooms full of farewell flowers, the command of "all visitors ashore," the sound of thunderous steam whistles, last-minute hugs, handkerchiefs waved at shipboard rails and dockside verandas, and a voyage across the sea aboard ships that were often considered to be "floating palaces." The *Queen Mary* (**above**) and *Queen Elizabeth* were great definitions of an ocean liners, maritime symbols of technology, speed, and luxury. They symbolized style, glamor, luxury, and extraordinary creature comfort. Hollywood, for example, often looked to the great ocean liners when a romantic, extravagant setting was demanded. As John Malcolm Brinnin wrote, "The whole milieu aboard these great ships was a 'buzz-for-the-masseuse' kind of thing." There were suites with private dining rooms, winter gardens and palm courts with fresh greenery, select grill rooms, and eight different kinds of bacon for breakfast on the *Queen Mary*.

Overleaf: The *Queen Mary* arriving at Pier 90, in a photo dated January 20, 1949, required no less than eight tugs for docking on this occasion. The Hudson's current was stronger than predicted, and the usual seven tugs needed an extra hand.

The Queens were not without problems, of course. Seen here (*above*) in a nighttime view at Southampton in 1949, the *Elizabeth* was not as well favored by the crew. She seemed to lack the warm chemistry and charm—beloved qualities that few ships seem to have from "within the wood panels"—that the *Mary* had radiated from the beginning. The *Mary* also enjoyed greater fame, being the first of the pair, a Blue Riband holder, and one of the very last liners with three funnels and therefore a throwback to a cherished, bygone era. The *Mary*, however, had her own blemishes. She suffered a common ill to many big liners: very strong vibrations. The ship's massive steel framework had to be reinforced, in fact, during her first winter overhaul back in January 1937. Extra steel beams had to be inserted, others strengthened, and the bilge keels widened. Whole lounges and cabins had to be stripped to bare steel in the process. Many of the fine, newly installed oak panels had to be removed, systematically numbered, stored ashore, and then reinserted. The original propellers were also found to be faulty and were replaced. The Cunarder was also a rather notorious, sometimes worrisome

roller, especially in those severe Atlantic gales. One colorful comment was that "the *Queen Mary* could roll the milk out of a cup of tea." One crewmember recounted, "I was thrown out of my bunk and thought the ship was never coming back, never righting herself. I thought this was the end! She can never come back from such a roll." On one early voyage, some passengers became hysterical as the liner rolled continuously. Heavy, hard rolling was a problem for the *Queen Mary* for most of her service.

The Queens were always thought of as a pair—even as sister ships or as twins. Many thought that they were identical. Instead, they were actually quite different ships. The *Mary* was a three-stacker, older, old-fashioned, and a speed champion; the *Elizabeth* had twin funnels, was more contemporary, raked, and perhaps slightly less grand. There is a charming story of a wealthy Texan dining in the Veranda Grill onboard the *Queen Mary*. So delighted with the food, the service, and in fact the entire ship, he asked if he might "buy" the liner. A rather surprised Cunard restaurant manager supposedly replied, "I'm terribly sorry, sir, but you see she's part of a set!"

Robin Davies began with Cunard as a waiter and then finished, nearly forty years later, as assistant hotel manager. "As a boy growing up in North Wales, I sometimes saw ships with streams of smoke coming from their funnels, and was intrigued. Thereafter, I always wanted to go to sea," he recalled. "There was no better firm than Cunard in those years, in the early 1950s. I started as a bellboy, in 1950, on the old, prewar *Ascania*, then serving on our Canadian trade between Liverpool and Quebec City. In those days, long before expensive labor and fast turnarounds, we'd spend as much as a week in port between voyages."

"Later, I transferred to the likes of the *Media*, the *Mauretania*, the *Caronia*, and to the illustrious *Queen Mary* and *Queen Elizabeth*," he remembered. "Onboard, the era of great luxury, of elegantly dressed gentlemen and fur-wrapped ladies, continued.

Personal servants collected jewels from strongboxes at the purser's office before dinner, for example. There were great private parties, six-course dinners with the captain, and bedclothes, as we called them, perfectly laid out when guests returned to their staterooms and suites. We did not just provide service, we created it. There was no request that went unfulfilled, nor an item that was considered too unimportant. Cunard service, and especially aboard the Queens, was equal to the finest hotels on shore, certainly the finest in London, as well as New York."

In this aerial view (*below*), dated 1956, the *Queen Elizabeth* is being docked on the north side of Pier 90, with another Cunarder, the *Scythia*, berthed at adjoining Pier 92. The stern section of the *Ile de France* is on the far right, with a freighter and the North German Lloyd's *Berlin* at the far top.

Here (***opposite, top***), the *Queen Elizabeth* is making an afternoon departure for Cherbourg and Southampton while the *Britannic* (right) will head out for Cobh and Liverpool. The date is May 14, 1958. Later that same year, in October, commercial jet aircraft will begin flying the Atlantic, and the great age of the Atlantic liner will begin its decline. Within six months, by mid-1959, the airlines would have two-thirds of all transoceanic traffic between the United States and Europe.

As the largest liners to visit New York in the 1950s, both the *Queen Elizabeth* (***opposite, bottom***) and *Queen Mary* needed the full 1,100-foot length of Pier 90. In fact, until the debut of the new French flagship *France* in 1962, the *Elizabeth*—at 1,031 feet from stem to stern—was the longest as well.

Like all ships, the Queens were occasionally delayed. Along with storms at sea, the ships had to contend with dockers' strikes, tugboat strikes, and icy conditions on the Hudson River during winter arrivals and departures. Here (***below***) we see Moran tugs carefully handling the inbound *Elizabeth* on February 11, 1958—a cold morning.

Sailing day was always a festive, crowded affair. On a peak summer sailing, the 2,000 passengers sailing on the *Queen Mary* (seen in this 1955 photo, **below**) or *Queen Elizabeth* could have as many as 5,000 relatives, friends, and boat enthusiasts waving farewells from the pier. Visitors had up to three hours before sailing to explore the ship, paying fifty cents for a boarding ticket, and were asked to go ashore thirty minutes before actual departure. Some well-wishers preferred to bid their good-byes from the large pier-side openings, while others stood on the balcony on the dock's outer end for a better view. Some patiently waited to see the liners all but disappear as they made their way down the lower Hudson.

A special occasion: the *Queen Mary* was dressed in flags as she headed down river on a July 1952 departure (**above**). The brand new *Flandre* (above the *Queen Mary*) is incoming from her maiden voyage, though her arrival was rather embarrassing for the French Line ship—she had broken down earlier in the day, in the Lower Bay, and so had to be towed by Moran tugs to her berth at Pier 88.

At Southampton, the brand new Ocean Terminal (***above***) was constructed especially for the Queens and opened in 1950, delayed by World War II. The structure included railway tracks underneath, which made for easy access to trains to and from London. The design of the Ocean Terminal (***opposite, top***), decorated in a 1930s Art Deco style, had a great similarity to the interiors of the liners themselves. Spacious and comfortable, it made for an easy transition between ship and shore. Facilities included a bar, newsstand, and florist.

At Cherbourg, the big Cunarders used the Gare Maritime, which had been damaged during the Second World War, but is seen undergoing repairs in this 1947 view (***opposite, bottom***) that includes the *Queen Elizabeth*.

In the late 1940s and '50s, the flawlessly maintained interiors of the *Queen Mary* and *Queen Elizabeth* exuded a timeless feel. They were classic ocean-liner style with British overtones (such as the use of burl woods and glossy linoleum floors), similar to the great hotels, skyscraper lobbies, and even those lavish, Depression-era Hollywood musicals. The main hall onboard the *Elizabeth* (**above**) was a most impressive space and, of course, a busy thoroughfare at sea and during arrivals and departures. Other grand spaces onboard the *Queen Elizabeth*, all for first-class travelers, include the Main Salon (**opposite, top**), the Observation Lounge and Cocktail Bar (**opposite, middle**), and the Garden Lounge (**opposite, bottom**), complete with fresh greenery.

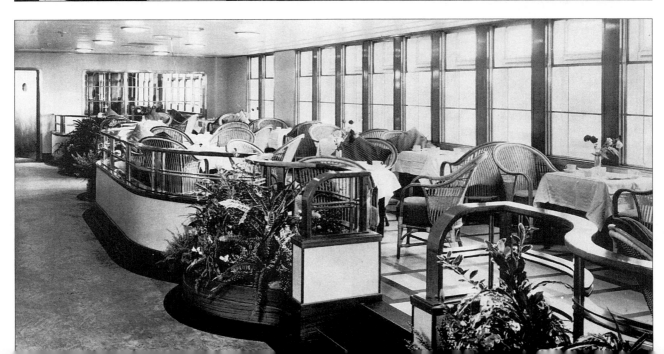

One of the *Elizabeth*'s most imposing spaces was undoubtedly her first-class main dining room (*above*). Done in Canadian maple, it sat 850 at one sitting. A sampling of the menus would show as many as 15 appetizers, 3 soups, 4 fish dishes, a farinaceous offering, a vegetarian item, 3 entrees, a sorbet, a meat joint (roast prime ribs of beef), a releve (roast Long Island duck), 3 grill items, 6 vegetables, 4 potatoes, 6 cold buffet items, 6 salads, 3 dressings, 5 sweets, 4 ice creams, 3 savoury items, fresh fruit, and coffee or tea.

"We had kings, queens, presidents, prime ministers and, of course, a near-endless parade of Hollywood stars, from the likes of Charlie Chaplin and Harold Lloyd to Elizabeth Taylor and Judy Garland," said Robin Davies, who served as a waiter on both Queens. "We had the Duke and Duchess of Windsor in the early 1950s, [shown *opposite, top*, sharing a table in the Veranda Grill onboard the *Queen Mary* with Lord Beaverbrook], Sir Winston and Lady Churchill several times [onboard the *Queen Elizabeth* in 1953, *opposite, bottom left*], and movie stars such as Madeline Carroll and her husband [on the *Elizabeth* in 1949, *opposite, bottom right*]." Other royal passengers, for example, included the Crown Prince of Japan, the king of Thailand, the exiled kings of Rumania and Yugoslavia, and Princess Mary (daughter of George V and Queen Mary). Queen Mary herself never traveled on either of the big Cunarders, but the late Queen Elizabeth The Queen Mother crossed to New York on the *Elizabeth* and then returned on the *Mary* in 1954.

MAURETANIA. Built just before start of World War II in 1939, the "second" *Mauretania* was often said to be a smaller version of the *Queen Elizabeth*. Both had two funnels, similar interior decor, and the same three-class passenger configuration. Used during the war as a troopship, the *Mauretania* (**above**) resumed sailing for Cunard in the spring of 1947. She was often said to be a "relief ship" for the Queens, filling in during their twice-annual dry dock periods, but this was not quite true. Being slower, she was not able to make five-day express crossings. Instead, she operated on a largely independent schedule: New York to Cobh in six days, or Le Havre and Southampton in seven. [Built by Cammell, Laird Shipbuilders Limited, Birkenhead, England, 1939. 35,655 gross tons in 1947; 772 feet long; 89 feet wide; 30-foot draft. Steam turbines, twin screw. Service speed 23 knots. 1,140 passengers (470 first-class, 370 cabin-class, 300 tourist-class).]

Seen here arriving in New York's Hudson River in 1958 (**opposite, top**), the *Mauretania*, though a very pleasant and well served ship, was not considered by Cunard to be in the same class as the

two Queens. First class onboard the larger liners was priced from $370 per person for five days in 1957. In comparison, a seven-day crossing on the *Mauretania* was considerably less expensive, being listed from $300. Week-long passages on the all-first-class *Media* began at $240. The lowest first-class fares of all ships that year were aboard the old veteran *Scythia*, with first-class accommodations beginning at $223 for her nine-day runs between New York and Liverpool.

Though in the shadow of her two grander sisters, the *Mauretania* occasionally made news, either for a famous passenger, a delayed arrival, or problems with strikes. In this view (**opposite, bottom**), dated March 27, 1954, the Cunarder is waiting at Pier 90 during a tug strike while Canadian Pacific's *Empress of Scotland* is mid-river and struggling to dock unassisted. After making three attempts that took over two hours, the *Empress* was finally able to dock. Delayed, the *Mauretania* undocked herself without tugs and then, happily, set sail for a two-week cruise to the Caribbean.

in summertime, and then back to the Mediterranean in the fall. Her shortest trip was about thirty days, her longest sometimes over 100. Named the *Caronia* (**above**), she was launched in October 1947 by Princess Elizabeth (later Queen Elizabeth II), seen here (**left**) with her husband, the Duke of Edinburgh to the right. She immediately made headlines: she was the largest postwar liner built in Britain, the largest yet with only one stack and one mast, and so luxurious that she was the first Cunarder to have a private bathroom in every cabin. She could also be used as a two-class ship—first- and cabin- but not tourist-class—for periodic positioning trips across the Atlantic in preparation for her New York cruise departures. Uniquely, she was painted in several shades of distinctive green and was soon dubbed "the Green Goddess." [Built by John Brown & Company Limited, Clydebank, Scotland, 1948. 34,183 gross tons; 715 feet long; 91 feet wide. Steam turbines, twin screw. Service speed 22 knots. 932 passengers (581 first-class, 351 cabin-class).]

The *Caronia* was "crowned" by the largest funnel yet to go to sea. Seen being topped-off at the John Brown shipyard on August 28, 1948 (**opposite**), the completed stack weighed 125 tons, measured 53 feet wide, and had a height of 46 feet.

CARONIA. Just after World War II ended, Cunard made plans for another liner as large as the *Mauretania*, but for the purpose of cruising rather than to make crossings. For eleven months of the year, she would sail on long, expensive luxury cruises: around the world each January, the Mediterranean in spring, Scandinavia

Dressed in flags and escorted by tugs, other harbor craft, and spraying fireboats, the *Caronia* arrived in New York for the first time in January 1949 (*above*). She berthed at Pier 90, just across from the *Queen Mary*. Two other passenger ships can be seen in this view: French Line's *De Grasse* at Pier 88 to the right, and the American-flag *Borinquen* just behind the *Queen Mary*, docked at Pier 92.

"It was Cunard policy in the 1950s to rotate [crew members] among the company's liners," recalled Robin Davies, who started as a bellboy and became, by 1986, assistant hotel manager on the *Queen Elizabeth 2*. "I served in most of their liners, but was very fortunate to have done eight around-the-world cruises in that most famous cruise ship of her day, the *Caronia*. I especially remember being aboard her in 1959, when we had to abruptly depart from Havana just as Fidel Castro was arriving. We had many, many special passengers aboard the *Caronia*, people who 'lived' onboard year after year. One woman was actually asked by her lawyers to remain out of the United States and instead to travel continuously on the ship. Another was so loyal that she lived in a small 'hut' at the dockside when the *Caronia* went into dry dock. She would simply not let the ship out of her sight."

Decoratively, the *Caronia*'s accommodations were very similar to both Queens and the *Mauretania*. There was a great sense of familiarity and continuity, which conservative-thinking Cunard directors felt were important, especially to the company's legions of repeat passengers. The elegant appointments were understated and comfortable, as visible here in the smoking room (**below**), with its masculine furnishings and dark tones.

The *Caronia* did not have the style and manner of a floating hotel, but rather, one of a floating country club. In these views, we see the Balmoral Restaurant (*opposite, top,* one of the two main dining rooms), and the 285-seat theatre (*opposite, bottom*). Although she could carry as many as 932 passengers, who were meticulously looked after by 600 crew, her cruise capacity was limited to 600. More often than not, she carried as few as 300 and 400 guests. "She was really just a large, luxurious, utterly magnificent yacht—not a liner like the others," remarked one woman who made no less than fifty trips with Cunard, a dozen of which were onboard the *Caronia*. Considered one of the finest liners afloat in the 1950s, it was said that Cunard used its best personnel to staff her. She offered world-class service and food, fine

entertainment, well-prepared shore excursions, and ever-changing, alluring itineraries. The millionaire set loved her.

The *Caronia* set the benchmark for big-ship luxury cruising until the early 1960s, when a new generation of cruise liners began to appear. Loyalists, both passengers as well as staff, stayed with her for years. Some felt that standards on the *Caronia* even exceeded first class on the *Queen Mary* and *Queen Elizabeth*.

At New York, the *Caronia* was occasionally included in some of those great gatherings of luxury liners along the city's West Side. In this aerial view from June 1960 (*above*), from top to bottom, are the *Media, Caronia, Queen Mary,* and *Britannic* of Cunard; the *Liberté,* French Line; the *America,* United States Lines; the *Saturnia,* Italian Line; and American Export Lines' *Constitution*.

BRITANNIC. The *Britannic*, one of the world's largest and most powerful motor liners of the 1930s, was the only member of the White Star Line to be restored for luxury service after the Second World War. Her near–sister ship, the *Georgic*, had been badly damaged, and though repaired and rebuilt, she served only as an austerity passenger ship beginning in the late 1940s, carrying troops, immigrants, and budget tourists. Sensibly, Cunard repainted the *Britannic's* squat funnels with her original White Star colors, thereby keeping something of the ship's former owner as a reminder to the traveling public and the maritime community. Seen here entering Liverpool's Gladstone Dock on March 13, 1948 (*above*), the liner is beginning the final stages of her restoration. She would be used on the Liverpool–New York run, calling at Cobh in each direction and occasionally at Halifax on the westbound passages. [Built by Harland & Wolff Limited, Belfast, Northern Ireland, 1930. 27,666 gross tons in 1948; 712 feet long; 82 feet wide. B&W type diesels, twin screw. Service speed 18 knots. 993 passengers in 1948 (429 first-class, 564 tourist-class).]

In this 1950 photo of the Cunard piers at Manhattan (*opposite, top*), the *Britannic* is on the left, loading a cargo of grain from two barges and a "floating grain elevator," one of New York harbor's more unique work craft. The *Queen Mary* is in the center and the *Mauretania* on the right. In total, the three liners would depart with over 4,000 passengers within that week.

Robin Davies, who sailed the *Britannic* as a waiter, noted, "I was on the final trip of the *Britannic* in December 1960. By then, she was the last of the White Star liners. She was a very elegant ship, especially in first class, and one that made huge profits for Cunard in the postwar years. She carried tens of thousands of immigrants to North America, especially Irish immigrants, who joined her at Cobh. In winter, she ran a two-month Mediterranean cruise from New York, but finishing at Southampton. Return fare to New York was included in the cost of the cruise. It was, of course, very select and quite an expensive trip in those days [fares from $950 for sixty days in 1959]. Consequently, on these trips, she attracted an older, well-traveled set of passengers. The atmosphere was like a great country house gone to sea." The *Britannic* is seen here (*opposite, bottom*) arriving at New York in a 1950s view from Battery Park, with the Statue of Liberty seeming to be one of her passengers.

GEORGIC. The *Georgic*, commissioned in June 1932 and White Star's last passenger ship, was heavily damaged while serving as a troopship in World War II. She was bombed by Nazi aircraft and set afire at Port Tewfik, Egypt, in September 1941, but despite considerable damage, was still worth saving. After extensive efforts, she finally reached Belfast in early 1943 and was repaired, but one of two funnels (the forward "dummy" stack) was removed. She became a full-time troopship in 1948, owned by the British Ministry of Transport, and began carrying immigrants as well, often to Australia.

Cunard, needing additional berths on the busy North Atlantic, chartered the *Georgic* (**above**) from 1950 through 1954. She offered inexpensive, all-tourist-class fares and sailed only in summers between Liverpool or Southampton, Le Havre, Cobh, Halifax (on the westbound voyages only), and New York. Because her wartime damages had left her unstable and partially unbalanced, she was not permitted, under the British Board of Trade regulations, to sail the Atlantic in winter. Instead, she made further immigrant trips out to Fremantle, Melbourne, and Sydney. Seen here at Cunard's Pier 92, she was finally scrapped in Scotland in 1956. Cunard, again in need of added berths, also chartered the 23,000-ton P&O liner *Stratheden* in 1950 for four sailings on the very busy Southampton–New York run. [Built by Harland & Wolff Limited, Belfast, Northern Ireland, 1932. 27,469 gross tons in 1950; 711 feet long; 82 feet wide. B&W type diesels, twin screw. Service speed 18 knots. 1,962 one-class passengers after 1948.]

MEDIA. "One of my favorite Cunard ships was the *Media*, a combination passenger-cargo ship with space only for 250 first-class passengers," remembered Robin Davies. "And we often carried less, sometimes as few as 50 or 100. Understandably, she was like a yacht. She was truly first class—with finger bowls at dinner, beef wagons, and crepes suzette. I recalled that actor Jack

Hawkins also preferred this type of more intimate ship as well. She sailed on the direct Liverpool–New York service, but occasionally we would detour to Norfolk, Virginia to load tobacco as well."

Initially intended to be large freighters for the Port Line, a Cunard subsidiary, the *Media* and her sister, the *Parthia*, were designed instead to assist the larger *Britannic* on the Liverpool–New York run, except with more freight and far fewer passengers. During her maiden voyage in August 1947 (seen here, **opposite, top**, arriving in New York's Upper Bay for the first time), the *Media* ranked as the first brand-new Atlantic passenger ship to be completed following World War II. Sweden's *Stockholm* was the second, arriving in the following winter. Never a very stable ship, Cunard engineers selected the *Media* for experimentation with new fin stabilizers. They were installed in January 1953, proved successful, and were quickly added to almost all other Cunard liners. [Built by John Brown & Company Limited, Clydebank, Scotland, 1947. 13,345 gross tons; 531 feet long; 70 feet wide. Steam turbines, twin screw. Service speed 18 knots. 250 all-first-class passengers.]

PARTHIA. A twin sister to the *Media*, the *Parthia* differed only in that she was built by Harland & Wolff at Belfast, an unusual shipbuilder for Cunard since they usually preferred John Brown in Scotland. The *Parthia* (**opposite, bottom**), seen here loading grain from a "floating grain elevator" just across from the *Queen Elizabeth*, usually spent up to six days in New York, arriving on Saturday and then sailing on the following Friday. On her seven-day direct passages between Liverpool and New York, she and the *Media* sometimes had detours: to Norfolk, Boston, and Bermuda. [Built by Harland & Wolff Limited, Belfast, Northern Ireland, 1948. 13,362 gross tons; 531 feet long; 70 feet wide. Steam turbines, twin screw. Service speed 18 knots. 250 all-first-class passengers.]

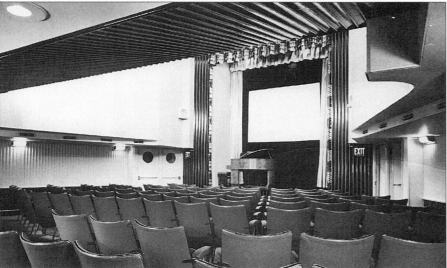

FRANCONIA. To maintain its alternate service to Eastern Canada, Cunard restored four of its prewar single-stackers: *Scythia, Samaria, Franconia,* and the smallest, *Ascania.* Beginning in the late 1940s, they sailed in tandem between London or Southampton, Le Havre, and Quebec City. In winters, when the St. Lawrence was closed, they ran to Halifax and sometimes down to New York as well. The *Franconia* (*opposite, top*), which had been a very popular luxury cruise ship in the prewar years, served as a troopship in World War II and as Winston Churchill's floating headquarters during the Yalta Conference in February 1945. She resumed Cunard sailings in June 1949, though she was creaking with age and sometimes less than operationally reliable. In particular, her steering mechanisms became faulty. Her officers dubbed her "the Frankenstein." After the new *Saxonia* class of four sister ships for the Canada service was introduced between 1954–57, these veteran liners from the 1920s deservedly went to the breakers. The *Franconia* was delivered to scrappers at Inverkeithing in Scotland in December 1956. [Built by John Brown & Company Limited, Belfast, Northern Ireland, 1923. 20,341 gross tons; 623 feet long; 73 feet wide. Steam turbines, twin screw. Service speed 16 knots. 1,050 passengers by 1949 (250 first-class, 800 tourist-class).]

ASCANIA. The *Ascania* was the smallest and the slowest of the postwar Canadian ships owned by Cunard. She also made occasional trips to New York, as seen in this view (*opposite, middle*). Her postwartime trooping service continued for three years, until 1948, and, after her lengthy restoration, she did not resume commercial sailings until April 1950. She endured until late 1956 and then, after a British government troop charter to Egypt for the Suez Crisis, was handed over to scrappers in Wales. [Built by Armstrong-Whitworth Company Limited, Newcastle-upon-Tyne, England, 1925. 14,440 gross tons in 1950; 538 feet long; 65 feet wide. Steam turbines, twin screw. Service speed 15 knots. 696 passengers in 1950 (198 first-class, 498 tourist-class).]

SAXONIA. To upgrade and reinforce its Canadian trade, Cunard built four new liners in the mid-1950s. In fact, they would be the last full transatlantic liners for the company. Their design was generally based on that of the 1948-built *Caronia,* using a single stack and single mast style. There were differences, however, such as the domed stack on the new quartet, increased cargo capacities, and two-class, Atlantic-style capacities with comparatively minimal first-class quarters and tourist-class dominance. The *Saxonia,* seen here during her trials in the summer of 1954 (*opposite, bottom*), was the first of the group. She had been named by Lady Churchill during her launching six months before. The *Saxonia* and the second sister, the *Ivernia,* were used in seasonal service from April through December, between London or Southampton, Le Havre, Quebec City, and Montreal. [Built by John Brown & Company Limited, Clydebank, Scotland, 1954. 21,367 gross tons; 608 feet long; 80 feet wide; 20-foot draft. Steam turbines, twin screw. Service speed 19.5 knots. 925 passengers (125 first-class, 800 tourist-class).]

The *Saxonia* and the *Ivernia* had especially modern interiors for Cunarders. Colors and tones were lighter, furniture was more modern, and public areas seemed brighter, larger, and more inviting. They contrasted sharply with the traditional darker, wood-paneled interiors normally found on Cunard passenger ships. In fact, the public was not all accepting of these new styles, and so the company decided to revert to more traditional, Cunard-style decor for the last set of these Canadian sisters, the *Carinthia* and *Sylvania.* Here we see the Choctaw Smoking Room (*left, top*) and the theatre aboard the *Saxonia* (*left, bottom*).

IVERNIA AND CARINTHIA. In winter, when the St. Lawrence was ice-clogged and all but closed to large ships, these newest Cunarders were routed to Halifax and then on to New York. As part of their crossings, two-night passages between New York and the Nova Scotia port were offered from $25 in tourist class and $40 in first class. During those winter sailings to New York, which were timed to a weekly service, these ships would remain in port for five to six days, primarily to handle cargos. But in this scene (*opposite, top*), dated December 11, 1959, two of the four are together at the same time at the Cunard piers. The *Ivernia* is at dock while the *Carinthia* is departing. [*Ivernia*: Built by John Brown & Company Limited, Clydebank, Scotland, 1955. 21,717 gross tons; 608 feet long; 80 feet wide; 28-foot draft. Steam turbines, twin screw. Service speed 19.5 knots. 925 passengers (125 first-class, 800 tourist-class). *Carinthia*: Built by John Brown & Company Limited, Clydebank, Scotland, 1956. 21,947 gross tons; 608 feet long; 80 feet wide; 28-foot draft. Steam turbines, twin screw. Service speed 19.5 knots. 868 passengers (154 first-class, 714 tourist-class).]

SYLVANIA. With the completion of the *Sylvania* (*opposite, bottom*), the new foursome for the Canadian service joined the Cunard fleet in May 1957. That winter, she even made several cruises to the Caribbean from New York, but Cunard designers had miscalculated. These new ships, without pools, lido decks, and too-few cabins with private bathrooms, were not suited for alternative, money-making service to the tropics. As the airlines overtook the steamship companies in 1957–58, transatlantic sailings began to decline and these Canadian liners, especially with their winter services, were among the first to struggle for passengers. By winter 1961, the *Carinthia* arrived at New York with a mere 180 passengers aboard. [Built by John Brown & Company Limited, Clydebank, Scotland, 1957. 21,989 gross tons; 608 feet long; 80 feet wide; 28-foot draft. Steam turbines, twin screw. Service speed 19.5 knots. 878 passengers (154 first-class, 724 tourist-class).]

In April 1961, following the retirement of the *Britannic* four months before and the decommissioning of the smaller *Media* and *Parthia*, Cunard rerouted the *Sylvania* off the declining Liverpool-Montreal service and moved her to Liverpool–New York sailings instead. This would last for another five years. The *Sylvania* is seen here (*above*) on the north side of Pier 92 in New York with the *Queen Mary* to its right at adjacent Pier 90.

ALSATIA. Cunard ran a separate cargo service across the Atlantic, sailing from the likes of Glasgow, Liverpool, and London over to New York, Boston, Philadelphia, Baltimore, and Norfolk. There were also sailings to Eastern Canada that included, after the opening of the St. Lawrence Seaway in 1959, ports along the Great Lakes. The company also ran a freighter service from Britain to the Mediterranean.

Two of the best known Cunard freighters of the 1950s and early '60s were the sisters *Alsatia* (*above*) and *Andria*, among the only twin-funneled cargo ships ever built (the forward stack was, in fact, a dummy and housed officers' quarters). They had been built in 1948 but by another British-flag shipowner, the Silver Line, as the *Silverplane* and *Silverbriar,* respectively. Cunard bought the pair in 1951 and generally used them on their London–New York

service. The *Alsatia* is seen here, in a scene from September 1957, loading heavy cargo at Brooklyn's Pier 30.

As Cunard turned more to chartered freighters, these sisters were sold off to the Chinese in 1963. The *Alsatia*, which became the *Union Freedom* for the Taiwan–New York run, was scrapped in the Far East in 1977. Cunard itself abandoned conventional, break bulk freighter operations in the late 1960s when they joined a new, transatlantic container consortium aptly called Atlantic Container Lines. One of their partners was, in fact, an old passenger ship rival, the French Line. [Built by J. L. Thompson & Sons Limited, Sunderland, England, 1948. 7,226 gross tons; 503 feet long; 64 feet wide. Steam turbines, single screw. Service speed 16 knots. 12 passengers as built.]

Chapter V

DECLINE, WITHDRAWAL, AND A NEW CUNARD

"Beginning in 1958–59, the airlines began to 'steal' our passengers and, rather quickly, all the transatlantic Cunarders were thereafter quite empty," remembered Robin Davies, then a steward rotating between most of the company's liners. "I recall one trip on the *Mary* when we had 500 passengers and 1,100 crew, and that was during a normally peak summer season crossing. On another trip, but in mid-winter, we had ninety on the *Carinthia*, which could carry as many as 875. We tried to put some of those 'grand ladies,' including the *Queen Mary* and *Queen Elizabeth*, into money-earning, tropical cruising such as New York down to Nassau, and Southampton to Las Palmas, but they were really not suited or as well equipped as the new generation of all-white, hotellike cruise ships."

"We tried feathers and paper flowers, and lively production shows," added Tony Dent, by then a member of the *Mary*'s new cruise staff in her twilight years. "But the age of bejeweled and fur-wrapped matrons was gone. The new, young, sun-seeking, rock 'n' roll dancing set had arrived, but did not seem to fit on those aged Cunarders."

The thirty-one-year-old *Queen Mary* was retired from Cunard's Atlantic service in September 1967 and shortly afterward was sold to the city of Long Beach, California for use as a floating hotel, convention center, museum, and carnival of shops and restaurants. Davies was aboard her last Cunard voyage, a long, senti-

mental journey from Southampton all the way to Los Angeles, sailing around the bottom of South America (she was too large to pass through the Panama Canal). "The trip was very nostalgic. Indeed, it was the end of an era," he reflected. "A violinist stood on a velvet-covered box in the dining room, for example, and played sentimental music. It was all very, very sad." Today, the *Mary* remains in southern California, a proud monument to the great liners of the past and, in fact, to the entire transatlantic passenger trade and its glorious history.

The *Elizabeth*, decommissioned a year later, in October 1968, was eventually sold to Chinese buyers, who refitted her as a combination cruise ship–floating university. She was renamed *Seawise University*. But, quite sadly, on the eve of her first departure from Hong Kong, in January 1972, several fires rather mysteriously broke out onboard. The blazing ship later capsized and her mangled remains were cut up for scrap metal. Those grand old Queens were no longer a royal pair. "The last crossings on ships like the *Queen Mary* was especially sad, deeply sentimental," remembered Davies, who had joined Cunard's sea-going staff in 1950. "There was great nostalgia, of course, on the beloved old *Mary*. I can recall the band in the Main Lounge and playing to rather few passengers. Those big lounges had grown very lonely."

In the twilight of a November afternoon in 1963, the two Queens met in a rare occasion at New York. The two giants passed one another in the Lower Bay (*opposite, top*). The *Mary* was inbound on an Atlantic crossing, the *Elizabeth* was off on a short cruise to the Bahamas. Cunard was beginning to struggle: Atlantic liner trade was on a steady, deeply worrisome decline, cruising was seen more and more as the future, shipboard labor and operational costs were rising, and Cunard's fleet was growing older and less competitive. The very modern, highly luxurious *France* arrived on the Atlantic run in February 1962, and the Dutch, Germans, and Italians had also added similarly trendy, up-to-date flagships. The Queens, with their old-fashioned, wood-paneled interiors, hinting more of the 1930s than the 1960s, were becoming dinosaurs. They began to lose money, as much as $4 million a year. The *Queen Mary* was already twenty-five years old, surely close to retirement for big ocean liners. Cunard directors were confident, if misguided, and began to plan for a replacement for the *Mary* that was dubbed Q3. She would be big and fast, and carry the traditional three classes of passengers. But the trend was already deeply toward two-class ships, still upper-deck first class and a larger, increasingly more comfortable tourist class. Cabin class, Cunard's "happy medium," had all but disappeared. The plans for the Q3 needed to be rethought and reworked. In due course the entire project was shelved. Instead, Cunard management and designers looked to a new idea, the so-called Q4 project.

BRITANNIC. Cunard began to downsize what was once the largest fleet on the Atlantic. At 30 years of age, the *Britannic* (*opposite, bottom*), which had mechanical troubles in the end, was sent off to the breakers in December 1960. She was the last of the White Star Line passenger ships, and so ended a great chapter in Atlantic passenger ship history. As a token, one of her steam whistles was given to the Liverpool Maritime Museum. "In the end, of course, the thirty-year-old *Britannic* was a victim of

pure old age," said Robin Davies. "She still had air chutes, for example, and six crew being squeezed into tiny cabins. Her operating costs were also too high and Cunard began to trim."

Within months, during 1961, the combination passenger-cargo liners *Media* and *Parthia* also went. The former was completely rebuilt as a 1,200-passenger Italian immigrant ship, the *Flavia*, for the still-lucrative Europe-Australia trade, and the latter stayed within the British fleet, joining the New Zealand Shipping Company as their *Remuera*. The 250-passenger *Media* and *Parthia* were replaced on the Liverpool–New York trade by two chartered Swedish freighters, which were specially renamed *Maronia* and *Naronia*. But Cunard accountants had still greater worries and concerns ahead.

MAURETANIA. In 1962, hoping to have a bigger share of the growing cruise industry, especially in the United States, Cunard repainted the veteran *Mauretania* (*above*) in so-called "cruising green," the distinctive hues associated with their legendary *Caronia*. Usually dressed in flags on the outside and given added decorative touches such as colored lights, plastic flowers, and cardboard murals, the *Mauretania* was sent off on a variety of leisure sailings: five days from New York to Bermuda, two and three weeks around the Caribbean islands, and longer, pricier trips such as four weeks to western Europe and six weeks through the Mediterranean. She also made charter trips, sailed from Southampton on leisure trips, and began winter service from a then-rapidly expanding cruise port: Port Everglades, Florida. In April 1963, Cunard was still searching for additional revenue and placed the *Mauretania* in a slightly different transatlantic service, between the Mediterranean and New York. It could not have been less successful. In this view at Southampton, in 1964, the *Mauretania*, dressed in flags, is already in her twilight years. The *Queen Mary* is at the left, at the Ocean Terminal.

The 1963–64 Cunard Mediterranean service between Naples, Genoa, Cannes, Gibraltar, and New York, was a great flop. The twenty-five-year-old *Mauretania*—dated and dark in tone—could not compete with the lively likes of the three-year-old *Leonardo da Vinci*, or the American liners *Independence* and *Constitution* on the same route. On some sailings, she carried as few as 200 to 300 passengers. Among her guests, however, was the Arison family, emigrating from Israel to the United States through Italy. In 1971, Ted Arison founded Carnival Cruise Lines, which grew to an unimaginable size in a short time, and which, in 1998, bought the entire Cunard company. By the fall of 1965, following a Mediterranean cruise that finished at Southampton, the *Mauretania* (**opposite, top**) became the next Cunarder to go. She arrived at Inverkeithing in Scotland on November 23 to begin demolition.

It should be noted that at this time, in 1965, Cunard had a 30 percent share in BOAC, the British Overseas Airways Company. Cunard had airline interests since 1962 with Cunard-Eagle Airways. In 1965, Cunard earned over $500,000 from its BOAC affiliation. But further changes were ahead. The devastating British seamen's strike in May and June of 1966 cost Cunard $4 million, coupled with the $14 million lost by their passenger division since 1961. Consequently, the shares in BOAC were sold off for well over $11 million by the end of 1966, the Liverpool headquarters was sold off a year later, and even the company's once-flourishing freighter subsidiary, the Port Line, posted its first losses.

CARONIA. The huge British maritime strike of May 1966 was devastating to, not only Cunard, but all national shipowners. Increased staff costs, for example, and heightened union demands caused Cunard to make further cuts. By the fall of 1967, the *Caronia*, the *Queen Mary*, and the *Carinthia* would be with-

drawn; the *Sylvania* and the *Queen Elizabeth* would go the following year. Cunard was losing millions, struggling on the Atlantic, but also forced into serious competition in both the American and British cruise markets. The *Caronia* was laid up in November 1967 and was to become a floating hotel along Yugoslavia's Dalmatian coast. However, she was sold to Greek buyers, the newly created Star Line (later renamed Universal Line), who rechristened as the *Caribia* for one- and two-week sailings from New York. Numerous problems, including a fire and breakdown on her inaugural trips, caused the ship to be towed back to New York, where it was laid-up for the next three and a half years. (**opposite, middle**, moored between Piers 84 and 86 in Manhattan in May 1971) Amidst deepening financial problems, she was finally sold for scrap in the spring of 1974 (shown (**opposite, bottom**) in her final New York berth, Cunard's former Pier 56, in a scene with the outbound cruise ship *Sea Venture* dated May 26, 1973). But she never reached shipbreakers in Asia: she wrecked on Guam in heavy weather, broke in three pieces, and was cut-up on the spot.

QUEEN MARY. By 1965–66, the crossings of the *Queen Mary* and the *Queen Elizabeth* were predictably reduced. Although somewhat ill-suited for the tropics, even the aging *Mary* was sent off on five-day vacation jaunts from New York to Nassau ($125 and up) and on week-long trips from Southampton to Las Palmas in the sunny Canaries. In Britain, these new roles for the once-proud Queens were seen as a demotion, even a degradation. They were mocked as "Cunard-on-Sea" (referring to cheap, holiday resorts), and as "Limping Leviathans." Some saw their decline as yet another indication of the fading of Britain. The *Mary* is seen here (**above**), on one of her last arrivals at New York, poetically silhouetted in the early morning light.

In 1966, with the new Q4 project underway at John Brown's yard in Scotland, company plans were to replace the thirty-year-old *Queen Mary* with the new 65,000-tonner. The *Elizabeth*, which had just had a costly $5 million refit to make her more suitable for cruising, would remain in service through "at least 1975," according to Cunard planners. But losses were mounting and, by late 1966, at an even faster rate. An inventive photographer has taken this view (*opposite, top*) of the *Queen Mary*'s foredecks from the crow's nest in her forward mast during one of her final arrivals at Cherbourg.

In May 1966, a message was dispatched to the masters of both Queens. It contained sad, but not entirely unexpected news. The *Mary* would be retired in September 1967, and the *Elizabeth* in October 1968. The era of those great Cunard Queens was coming to an end. The news was soon made public, resulting in a surge in passengers. Special tours were organized aboard the legendary ships, such as with this group in the first-class dining room on the *Queen Mary* (*above*). At New York, Cunard thoughtfully scheduled "open house" days during layovers at Pier 92 so former passengers, service men from World War II, maritime enthusiasts, the nostalgically curious, and even budding 1930s and Art Deco buffs could visit. Floating monuments to a largely bygone era, the two Queens were pictures of faded splendor, the interiors turned slightly shabby, the mood forlorn.

Expectedly, there were more passengers than usual aboard the *Queen Mary*'s final sailing from New York on September 22, 1967. Many wanted that last chance to cross the Atlantic on that famed ship. Captain Treasure Jones offers a toast in the Main Lounge on that final departure day (*opposite, bottom*).

A flotilla of harbor craft, tugs, fireboats, specially chartered excursion vessels, and pleasure craft, along with overhead helicopters and small planes escorted the *Queen Mary* on that final departure. She is seen here (*above*) passing Lower Manhattan, making her way for the last time in the lower reaches of the Hudson River. She had a most impressive record: 1,001 crossings and some two million passengers carried since 1936. She was also the very last three-stacker. But Cunard was optimistic — on September 20, two days before, Queen Elizabeth II had named the *Queen Elizabeth 2* in a highly publicized launching from the same slipway at Clydebank where both the *Mary* and original *Elizabeth* had been created. This ship, quickly dubbed the *QE2*, was to be the future, according to Cunard's new management.

Initially, the *Queen Mary* had an uncertain future after her

days with Cunard. Far Eastern scrappers were interested, of course, but so were others. An Australian syndicate wanted her for Southampton-to-Sydney immigrant service, Gibraltar investors envisioned her as a moored casino, and even New York City considered making her a floating public high school berthed along the Brooklyn waterfront. But it was the city of Long Beach, California, rich in harbor oil monies, that bought her for $3.2 million and decided that she would make the ideal harbor attraction: hotel, restaurants, shops and, of course, a museum. And so, on October 31, 1967, she set off from Southampton, as seen here from waterside Mayflower Park (*opposite*), on a five-week cruise to her new Southern California home via Brazil, the Straits of Magellan, Chile, Peru, Panama, and the Mexican Riviera.

After reaching her new California home port in December 1967, the *Queen Mary* underwent an extensive, $72 million transformation from active, sea-going passenger liner to a permanently moored museum, hotel, and collection of ships. Now officially a "building," she opened in May 1971. But while never a huge success, she has endured to this day (***top***). A recreated English village was built alongside, and the "Spruce Goose," the great flying boat created by Howard Hughes, was added to the site in 1981 (it was sold and moved ten years later). Soon after, in the early 1990s, there was a short-lived plan to lease the *Queen Mary* for several years to the city of Tokyo, thereby raising enough money through leasing fees to improve and repair the former Cunard Line flagship. The project, however, never materialized. In 2003, Carnival Cruise Lines, by then the parent of Cunard itself, opened a new cruise terminal adjacent to the *Queen Mary* at Long Beach. Costing $40 million, it allows Carnival cruise ships to use the three-stacker for boarding and disembarkation procedures, as well as for tours and hotel packages. The project gave new life to the once-mighty *Queen Mary*.

QUEEN ELIZABETH. This scene (***middle***), from 1965, depicts one of the very last gatherings of the great Atlantic passenger ships along New York City's "Luxury Liner Row": from top to bottom are the *Constitution*, American Export Lines; *United States*, United States Lines; *France*, French Line; *Raffaello*, Italian Line; and the *Queen Elizabeth*.

In November 1968, at twenty-eight years old, the *Queen Elizabeth* followed the *Mary* into retirement. The month before, dressed in flags and surrounded by an outbound flotilla of harbor craft, small boats, and overhead helicopters, she sailed off on her final crossing (seen here in this aerial view, ***bottom***). Her record was as impressive as her sister's: 907 Atlantic crossings, 3,470,000 miles steamed, and 2,300,000 passengers in peace and war. Queen Elizabeth The Queen Mother paid a farewell visit to the ship that she had named thirty years before. It was planned that the liner would be sold to Philadelphia for use as a hotel, museum, and general tourist attraction, but plans changed. Instead she was sent to Port Everglades, Florida, arriving there on December 8. Fading in the Florida sun, the project to convert the *Elizabeth*, similar to the *Mary* on the Pacific coast, failed to materialize due to mismanagement, poor planning, and—most of

all—little or no money. By 1970, the *Queen Elizabeth* was bankrupt. She was seized by local authorities, auctioned for debt that September, and, for $3.2 million, was sold to the Seawise Foundation, an arm of the rapidly expanding, Hong Kong–based C. Y. Tung shipping empire. Tung's Orient Overseas Line was then becoming one of the largest and most profitable merchant fleets in the world. The *Elizabeth* set off on a long, arduous journey to Hong Kong via Capetown in February 1971, and then began a lengthy, costly refit to become the *Seawise University*, the world's first combination university-cruise ship. She would make cruises, transpacific voyages, and even a seventy-five-day around-the-world trip that would bring her back to New York in the fall of 1972.

On the eve of her first scheduled voyage for C. Y. Tung, with her refit all but complete, a devastating fire broke out on the former *Elizabeth*. As many as eight different blazes raged on the ship anchored in Hong Kong harbor on January 8, 1972 (*above*). As the fires turned into an inferno and swept the giant ship, she blistered into a mass of twisted, collapsed steel, later becoming overloaded with firefighters' water and finally capsizing (*left, top*). The last fire was not extinguished until five days later (*left, bottom*). A Dutch salvage company considered refloating the remains, but in the end, Japanese scrappers cut up the badly bruised hulk on the spot. The *Queen Elizabeth* was gone. All that remained to commemorate her memory were two large letters—Q and E—taken from her bow and installed as an outdoor sculpture-memorial in front of C. Y. Tung's offices along Lower Manhattan's Water Street.

CARMANIA. In 1967–68, well before the two Queens were retired, Cunard was rethinking its fleet and deployments. Two wise decisions were made in the fall of 1962, when the traditional, Atlantic-styled *Saxonia* and *Ivernia* (the first two of the Canadian foursome built in 1954–57) were extensively refitted. Their accommodations were upgraded, new public rooms added, private bathrooms installed, and a lido deck with oval pool built in place of the ship's aft three cargo holds. They were repainted in Cunard's so-called "cruising green" as vivid reminders of the ultra-luxurious *Caronia*, and even given new identities: the *Saxonia* became the *Carmania* and *Ivernia* changed to *Franconia*. Their transatlantic schedules were hereafter abbreviated to April through October, while the remainder of the year was spent in lucrative cruising, the *Carmania* from Port Everglades, Florida and the *Franconia* from New York. Crossings were extended to include Rotterdam, where the *Carmania* is seen in this view dated September 1965 (*above*), for the convenience

of Continental passengers. Both ships were successful; portions of their architecture were even adopted by the Q4 project, which was still in design stages. [Built by John Brown & Company Limited, Clydebank, Scotland, 1954. 22,592 gross tons as rebuilt in 1963; 608 feet long; 80 feet wide; 28-foot draft. Steam turbines, twin screw. Service speed 19.5 knots. 881 passengers as refitted in 1963 (117 first-class, 764 tourist-class).]

FRANCONIA. The interiors of these two Cunarders had a pleasant, comfortable style. Here we see the main lounge (*opposite, top*) and an outside double-bedded stateroom (*opposite, bottom*) onboard the *Franconia*. [Built by John Brown & Company Limited, Clydebank, Scotland, 1955. 22,637 gross tons as refitted in 1963; 608 feet long; 80 feet wide; 28-foot draft. Steam turbines, twin screw. Service speed 19.5 knots. 847 passengers as refitted in 1963 (119 first-class, 728 tourist-class).]

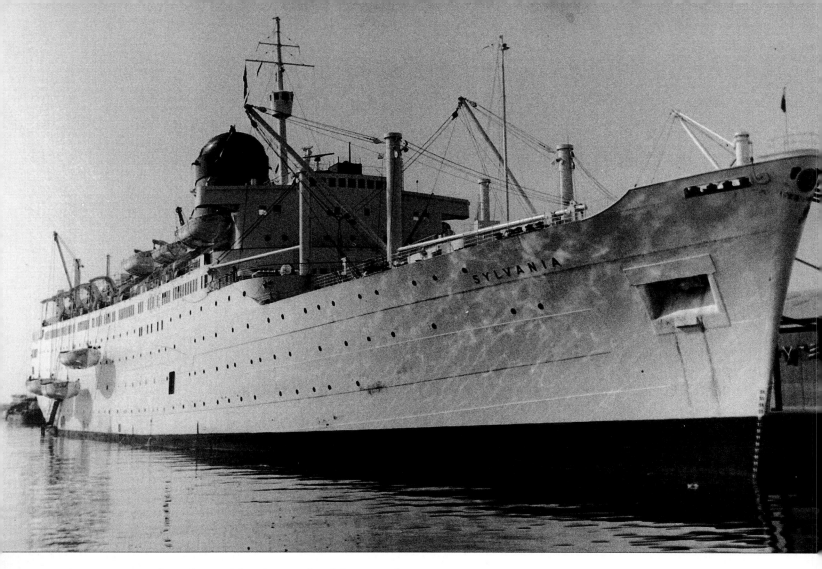

SYLVANIA. The *Sylvania* (**above**) was refitted for more alternate, off-season cruising in December 1966, after closing out Cunard's century-old Liverpool–New York service a month before. In October 1967, her sister, the *Carinthia*, closed out another long-established, company link, the Liverpool–Canada service. The company had moved its headquarters to Southampton, and thereafter all Atlantic crossings would be concentrated there. The *Sylvania* was given new tenders, a more colorful showroom, and was repainted in all-white. A month later, she left Liverpool on a twenty-seven-day cruise around the Mediterranean (seen here at Gibraltar). It was the first Cunard cruise from that Mersey River port since 1939.

DAWN PRINCESS. Needing extensive refits to continue successfully in the British cruise trade, both the *Carinthia* and *Sylvania* were laid-up by Cunard in 1968 and were quickly sold. The Monte Carlo–based Sitmar Line wanted to expand its Europe-Australia liner business and so bought the pair, which were renamed *Fairland* and *Fairwind* respectively. But with Sitmar's bid to enter the expanding American market, the ships were ultimately converted for cruising. The ships were lavishly rebuilt at Trieste (with 910 all-first-class berths each), and the *Fairland* was more suitably renamed *Fairsea*. They were hugely successful, sailing to the likes of the Caribbean, the Mexican Riviera, and to Alaska in summertime. When Sitmar was sold to P&O-Princess Cruises in 1988, the pair was absorbed: the *Fairsea* became the *Fair Princess* and the *Fairwind* changed to *Dawn*

Princess (**opposite, top**). The *Dawn Princess* was sold in 1993, and continues to run German charter cruises as the *Albatros* until scrapped in 2004; the *Fair Princess* became the Far East–based *China Sea Discovery* in 2000.

FEODOR SHALYAPIN. The other two ships of the Cunard Canadian foursome, the *Carmania* (ex-*Saxonia*) and *Franconia* (ex-*Ivernia*), remained in Cunard service until late 1971. They were laid-up and offered for sale, with interested buyers that included the Japanese, the Greek-owned Chandris Lines, and even a brand-new company that planned to call itself Carnival Cruise Lines. In the end, it was the Soviets, through their Odessa-based Black Sea Steamship Company, that bought the pair and renamed them the *Leonid Sobinov* and *Feodor Shalyapin* (**opposite, bottom**, departing from Lisbon). Afterward, they made charter cruises for Western companies, carried students and sports teams to Cuba, shipped troops to assorted locations, and even ran tourist sailings between Europe and Australia. In 1992, following the collapse of the Soviet Union, they retained their names but shifted to Maltese-flag ownership. Both were laid-up in 1996, with the *Leonid Sobinov* going to Indian breakers in October 1999. The *Feodor Shalyapin* followed four years later, ending her days at Alang, India.

At the time that the *Carmania* and *Franconia* were being retired from the fleet, Cunard itself was sold, bought out for $26 million by Trafalgar House Investments, a huge holding organization with no less than 260 subsidiary companies.

Chapter VI

ROYAL SUCCESSORS: *QUEEN ELIZABETH 2* AND *QUEEN MARY 2*

Friday, July 27, 1990 was a very special birthday for what remained one of the best known names in shipping—Cunard was 150 years old. And what better way to celebrate than with a fleet review, bands, fireworks, spraying fireboats, a flyover by the Concorde, and an appearance by none other than Her Majesty Queen Elizabeth II.

I was traveling onboard the *Vistafjord*, the former Norwegian America cruise ship, which was then part of Cunard's fleet. We were due to join the festivities, scheduled to begin at nine in the morning off Spithead in the very south of England, just across from the big naval base at Portsmouth and about an hour's sailing from Southampton, that famed ocean liner port. The 24,000-ton *Vistafjord* looked especially resplendent: her dove-gray hull gleaming, flags strung from end to end, her Cunard orange-red and black funnel colors freshly painted. As we 700 passengers and most of the crew lined the outer decks, we dropped anchor at an exact, prearranged spot just across from two far bigger ships, the boxlike, imposing, 59,000-ton containership *Atlantic Conveyor* (also Cunard-owned) and the ever-majestic *Queen Elizabeth 2*. Together we formed the port side fleet while a string of smaller vessels, mostly military, made up the starboard collection. Fittingly, with this maritime gathering seemingly set to exacting precision, the threatening gray skies cleared. Then, almost on stage cue, the most honored guest of the day arrived.

The Queen, accompanied by Prince Philip, traveled out in the royal yacht *Britannia*, a 6,000-ton floating palace that had left Portsmouth earlier and was ceremoniously led by a sparklingly fit lighthouse tender, the *Patricia*. The three-masted yacht looked especially regal: her colorful banners and dress flags fluttering, impeccably uniformed sailors lining the outer decks in perfect formation, and the ship's flawlessly enameled marine-blue hull reflecting off the waters of the Solent. Amidst cheers and applause, the royal party sailed through the center formation of assembled craft, then came closer for a better look. A small

woman in a green dress and matching hat waved to us with a white-gloved hand. Horns honked and sirens blared. An air review followed: the Concorde, a Harrier, and a vintage British Airways Comet.

Later, the Queen boarded the *QE2* for a more official welcome. The leisurely, three-hour sail to Southampton would be, in fact, Her Majesty's first voyage in the ship she had named at Clydebank in September 1967. At lunch, there were toasts, dedications, and the exchange of commemorative gifts. There was also a blazing rumor about that, along with dessert, the Cunard chairman would announce the building of an 85,000-tonner, the so-called "next generation transatlantic super ship," which would do faster, four-day crossings and which, it was also rumored, had been dubbed the "Queen Diana." But the rumor proved to be just that. There was no mention, at least in Her Majesty's presence, of a big, new, successive Cunarder. After lunch, the Queen toured the *QE2*'s public rooms, met a collection of retired Cunard skippers, and posed for the obligatory photos on the port side of the bridge wing.

It would take at least another dozen years before a new Cunard "super ship" was actually in the works. Construction of the 150,000-ton *Queen Mary 2* was well underway, but—in a rather strange twist of history—in France. She was being built at the very same yard where, seventy years before, the *Normandie* had been constructed. Just as it was in the 1930s, when Cunard made headlines by producing not one but two of the largest, fastest, and greatest liners yet built, the company was again making important news. The *Queen Mary 2* would be the biggest, most expensive, and most lavish ocean liner ever to put to sea. And so, the legacy of the original *Queen Mary* and *Queen Elizabeth* would continue. Grandly inherited and carried on by the *Queen Elizabeth 2*, the "crown" of the Cunard Queens now has been passed to the *Queen Mary 2*. Proudly, the great story of these great ships continues!

Right: The joyous launch of the *Queen Elizabeth 2* on September 20, 1967.

QUEEN ELIZABETH 2. After Cunard directors had scrapped the idea of a traditional, three-class superliner (the Q3) by 1964, they planned instead a more modern, two-class liner—the Q4—with easy adaptability between half-year crossings and half-year cruising. She would be fast, but not a record-breaker (there was simply no need by the 1960s). Not quite as big as the veteran *Queen Mary* and *Queen Elizabeth*, she would also do away with many Cunard traditions, such as staid, traditional decor. Instead, the Q4 would be modern, very contemporary, and even futuristic. Naming her was a major issue. By 1965, there were many rumors afloat: "Britannia," "Winston Churchill" (who had just died in January 1965), "British Queen," "British Tourist," and even "John F. Kennedy" (tragically assassinated in 1963, his name was considered a strong link to the largely American clientele). "Queen Mary" was also said to be a strong contender. Queen Elizabeth II had agreed to do the naming at the ship's launch on September 20, 1967 and, in discussion with Cunard officials, agreed on *Queen Elizabeth 2*. The new ship was named after the previous liner, not the current queen. [Built by Upper Clyde Shipbuilders Limited (formerly John Brown & Company Limited), Clydebank, Scotland, 1965–69. 65,863 gross tons as built; 963 feet long; 105 feet wide; 32-foot draft. Steam turbines, twin screw. Service speed 28.5 knots. 2,005 passengers as built (564 first-class, 1,441 tourist-class).]

"Ships have been boring long enough," declared a Cunard advertisement heralding the company's new flagship. The established Cunard image was to be overhauled with the *Queen Elizabeth 2*, which was hailed as a modern ship (or "floating hotel") for contemporary travelers. John Brown, her builder, planned to deliver her to Cunard that November (this 1968 photo, ***opposite, top***, shows the wheelhouse and bridge sections being lifted aboard). Her trials would include a shakedown cruise, final touches, and then her three-week maiden voyage from Southampton to the Caribbean in January 1969. But near-continuous problems surfaced: during her sea trials, serious turbine problems and other defects were found and Cunard refused to accept delivery. In January, despite modifications and then further testing, Cunard again refused. The maiden voyage, all winter

sailings, and some spring trips were canceled amidst harsh publicity, disappointing thousands of passengers. Finally, after another set of trials held in March, during which the ship reached 32.66 knots, Cunard was finally ready. On April 18, the *QE2* officially passed into her rightful ownership. The delays, changes, and cancellations had cost some $10 million. On May 2, she left New York on a gala five-day crossing direct to New York. The headlines and accompanying news stories finally became positive.

As the *QE2* sailed along the River Clyde for the first time in November 1968, bound for her first sea trials, among the guests was Prince Charles (***opposite, bottom left***). His mother, Queen Elizabeth II, had named the new Cunard flagship at the launching in September 1967, and she herself would visit in April 1969.

"When the *QE2* was built, 10 percent [more reinforcement in the steel] was added to her strength by Cunard, and then the John Brown shipyard added another 10 percent," reported Knut Aune, Cunard's assistant vice president in the 1980s. "The *QE2* has enormous strength. Her steel is a little less than 1.5 inches thick, which is far greater than any other liner these days. Most ships would sink when she never did. She is designed and built based on long experience in marine design, engineering, and construction. There's nothing like her these days. Today, ships are built by computer." This photo (***opposite, bottom right***) shows the ship during her spring sea trials in 1969.

As a symbol of the revival—or at least a continuation—of the transatlantic liner trade, the *Queen Elizabeth 2* arrived in New York to an especially joyous welcome in May 1969. She is seen here (***above***) approaching Lower Manhattan. "For me, even to this day, she is a ship of enormous history," remarked Aune proudly. "She has had a great career. I see her this way and greatly respect her."

Frank Trumbour, a former president of the Ocean Liner Museum Project at New York added, "The *QE2* has a very proud place in history. Even with her replacement by the *Queen Mary 2*, she will truly be the last in many ways. In the *QE2*, you can still see the continuity from the original *Queen Mary* and *Queen Elizabeth*. The *QE2* is very much the last of the great ocean liners."

Beginning in 1975, a series of refits, modernizations, and extensions began on the *QE2*. Suites, for example, were added to the uppermost decks (**above**) during a winter refit in 1975 at Bayonne, New Jersey.

In October 1986, the *QE2* made the last Atlantic passage, from New York to Southampton, under steam. Afterward, she was sent to Bremerhaven, West Germany and underwent an extensive, very expensive conversion to diesel-electric engines. This made her more efficient, and extended her operational life as well. "The transplant on the *QE2* has allowed the ship to endure to thirty-four years [2003]," noted Aune. "The original steam plant was worn out. The conversion to diesel was life-saving in every way to that great ship." The *QE2* resumed sailing in May 1987 and her "new look" included a wider, broader funnel that, to many, has enhanced her exterior. She is seen here (**below**) passing through the Panama Canal in 1995.

From the time following her maiden voyage, the *QE2* has divided her schedule between crossings (April through December) and cruises. Here we see the Cunard flagship during a summertime cruise to Scandinavia (***above***), sailing from Copenhagen on June 10, 1992. On the left, at dock, are the *Seabourn Pride* and the larger *Royal Princess*. "To this day [2003], the *QE2* has armies of fans and loyalists," commented Trumbour. "She is maintained beautifully. She has a renewed freshness about her and she is looking better than ever, both inside as well as out. To sail aboard her is a great experience, certainly one of the finest travel experiences. Her food and service are very good and to dine in the Queens Grill is today's epitome of the great ocean liner experience."

On the evening of August 29, 2002, the *QE2* reached a unique milestone: she had sailed her five millionth nautical mile. No other liner has had a comparable record. She is seen here (***left***), in a view dated April 2001, outbound from New York for Southampton and passing the World Trade Center.

101

CUNARD ADVENTURER AND CUNARD AMBASSADOR.
By the late 1960s, Cunard directors saw mass-market cruising as a positive investment. They soon bought a 50 percent share in a new cruise project begun by Overseas National Airways, a charter airline that included no less than six 14,000-ton, mass-market cruise ships. When Overseas National ran into financial difficulties and had to abandon its share, Cunard took over the project, which was then conservatively reduced to two ships. The company commissioned the twin sister ships, the *Cunard Adventurer* (shown berthed at San Juan, Puerto Rico, **opposite, top**) and the *Cunard Ambassador* (seen in dry dock at Hoboken, New Jersey on June 2, 1973, **opposite, bottom**) primarily for popular seven-day cruises: New York to Bermuda, San Juan to other Caribbean ports, and, in summer, Vancouver to Alaska. Too small to suit Cunard accountants, they were soon replaced by a larger pair, the *Cunard Countess* and *Cunard Princess*.

The *Cunard Ambassador* caught fire in September 1974 off the Florida coast while on a positioning trip, and therefore without passengers. Declared a loss, she was sold to Danish interests and rebuilt as the sheep carrier *Linda Clausen*. She burned again, however, while in the Indian Ocean in July 1984. This time, she was beyond economic repair and, at age thirteen, was sold to Taiwanese ship breakers. The *Cunard Adventurer* remained with Cunard until 1976, when she was sold to Norwegian Cruise Lines (then called Norwegian Caribbean Lines), who sailed her as the *Sunward II*, before being sold again, in 1991, to Greece's Epirotiki Lines, who renamed her *Triton*. She remained in Greek cruise service until December 2003, but under the reorganized banner of Royal Olympic Cruises. Those owners were forced into bankruptcy at that time, and the ship was then auctioned to other owners. [*Cunard Adventurer* (1971) and *Cunard Ambassador* (1972): Each built by Rotterdam Dry Dock Company, Rotterdam, Netherlands, 1971. 14,155 gross tons; 484 feet long; 71 feet wide. Diesels, twin screw. Service speed 20.5 knots. 806 all-first-class passengers.]

CUNARD COUNTESS.
With the *Cunard Adventurer* and *Cunard Ambassador* proving less than successful (being too small and inefficient, and suffering from mechanical problems almost from the start), larger and improved versions were planned by 1975. In August 1976, the company introduced the *Cunard Countess* (shown here on her sea trials, **above**) and the *Cunard Princess* (first named *Cunard Conquest*) in the following March. They were rather unique creations, being built primarily in Denmark but then towed around Western Europe to Italy for fitting-out and final completion. Like their predecessors, both were designed for the growing seven-day air-sea cruise trade. The *Cunard Countess* ran seven-day Caribbean cruises from San Juan; the *Cunard Princess* divided her time at first between seasonal (April–October) New York–Bermuda sailings and weekly Caribbean trips from Port Everglades, Florida for the remainder of the year. [Built by Burmeister & Wain Shipyards, Copenhagen, Denmark; completed by Industrie Navali Mechaniche Affine Shipyard, La Spezia, Italy, 1976. 17,495 gross tons; 536 feet long; 74 feet wide. B&W type diesels, twin screw. Service speed 20.5 knots. 750 all-first class passengers.]

CUNARD PRINCESS. While British royalty have traditionally been associated with Cunard naming ceremonies and launchings, the honors for the *Cunard Princess* went to Princess Grace of Monaco (*opposite, top*). The ceremonies were even more distinctive: she was the first liner to be named at New York City piers. Cunard announced at that time that the 17,000-ton *Cunard Princess* would probably be the last new cruise ship ever built. Fuel oil prices were overtaking profits, and cruising seemed to have reached a saturation point. Within two years, however, by 1979, the mood began to change and there were signs of further growth. Like other companies, Cunard watched closely. [Built by Burmeister & Wain Shipyard, Copenhagen, Denmark; completed by Industrie Navali Mechaniche Affine Shipyard, La Spezia, Italy, 1977. 17,496 gross tons; 536 feet long; 74 feet wide. B&W type diesels, twin screw. Service speed 20.5 knots. 750 all-first-class passengers.]

The twins *Cunard Countess* and *Cunard Princess* (*opposite, bottom*), seen here together at San Juan, Puerto Rico, were very successful during the nearly twenty years spent with Cunard. They represented a good balance of moderate size and the amenities and comforts suited to the new age of air-sea, seven-day cruising. The *Cunard Princess* was the first Cunarder liner to use non-British registry when she was transferred to the Bahamian flag in October 1980. The *Cunard Princess* was sold in January 1995 to Italy's Starlauro Cruises, becoming their *Rhapsody*, a cruise ship for summers in the Mediterranean and winters on charters in either South American or South African waters. Later that same year, she was sold to Mediterranean Shipping Company, but for the same cruise schedules and under the same name. The *Cunard Countess* was bought in October 1996 by Indonesian interests and renamed *Awani Dream 2* for cruising in the East. But her owners were soon bankrupt, and by 1998, she was sold to Greece's Royal Olympic Cruises and renamed *Olympic Countess* (a name modified in 2001 to *Olympia Countess*). At the time of writing, she sails the Eastern Mediterranean for about half the year, and in Caribbean waters for the remainder. After Royal Olympic fell into bankruptcy in December 2003, she was auc-tioned off for debt to another Greek company, Majestic International Cruises, and renamed *Ocean Countess*.

SAGAFJORD. By the early 1980s, Cunard was looking to expand. Mergers and acquisitions became increasingly common and the Cunard name was linked to Royal Caribbean Cruise Lines, Sitmar Cruises, and P&O Cruises. In 1983, for $73 million, Cunard bought the highly reputed Norwegian America Cruises and their two luxury cruise liners, the *Sagafjord* and *Vistafjord*. They were especially noted for their long, luxurious voyages and seemed an ideal continuation to the legacy of the *Caronia*. Initially, there was a plan to integrate them fully into the Cunard fleet by renaming them "Aquitania" and "Mauretania" respectively, but the idea was quickly shelved and their original, well known names were retained under the Cunard-Norwegian America Cruises banner. High standards continued and, by 1985–86, the *Sagafjord* (seen here departing from San Francisco, *above*) was rated as the finest cruise ship afloat, gaining an unparalleled 5 1/2 stars in at least one well-read guide book. The two ships followed ever-changing patterns, from two-night cruises to nowhere out of New York, to two weeks to Scandinavia from Hamburg, and as long as 100 days completely around-the-world. They were so popular, they had repeater rates that exceeded 70 percent on some voyages.

Unfortunately, the *Sagafjord* had a fire and breakdown in the Philippines during her world cruise on February 26, 1996, and her Cunard days were numbered. Later repaired, she began a charter that summer to Germany's Transocean Tours as the *Gripsholm*, using a legendary cruise ship name from the defunct Swedish American Line. Less than a year later, in 1997, she was sold off completely, going to Britain's Saga Cruises and being refitted as their *Saga Rose*. In 2003, she was roaming the world on Saga itineraries. [Built by Societe des Forges et Chantiers de la Mediterranee, Toulon, France, 1965. 24,002 gross tons; 615 feet long; 82 feet wide. Sulzer diesels, twin screw. Service speed 20 knots. 789 all-first-class passengers.]

VISTAFJORD. A near-sister to the *Sagafjord*, the slightly larger *Vistafjord* (**opposite, top**) divided her schedule between the German-European cruise market out of Hamburg and Genoa, and the remainder of the year in the North American trade, usually from Port Everglades, Florida. Although never quite as beloved as the *Sagafjord*, the *Vistafjord* was nevertheless extremely popular and often booked to capacity. She is seen here, on July 27, 1990, during Cunard's 150th anniversary review off Spithead. The royal yacht *Britannia* is approaching, and the company-owned containership *Atlantic Conveyor* is off to the upper right. In December 1999, she was renamed *Caronia* in something of a fleet reorganization for Cunard. All links to the ship's original Norwegian America heritage seemed to be severed. The ship itself was retired from the Cunard fleet in October 2004 and sold to another British company, Saga Cruises. After a lengthy refit and renaming, she will join her onetime fleetmate, the *Saga Rose* (ex-*Sagafjord*), in worldwide cruising. [Built by Swan Hunter Shipbuilders Limited, Newcastle-on-Tyne, England, 1973. 24,292 gross tons; 628 feet long; 82 feet wide. Sulzer diesels, twin screw. Service speed 22 knots. 600 maximum cruise passengers.]

BRITANNIA. Her Majesty Queen Elizabeth II and Prince Philip (**opposite, bottom**) peer from the aft deck of the yacht *Britannia* to the flag-bedecked *Vistafjord*, her outer decks lined with passengers and crew. Later, the Queen would travel by launch to the nearby *QE2* and join that ship for lunch, ceremonies, and the three-hour sail along the Solent to Southampton.

SEA GODDESS TWINS. Cunard expanded its luxury cruise division in 1986, when a twelve-year charter was arranged for the cruising yachts *Sea Goddess I* (seen here anchored off the Greek island of Mykonos, **above**) and *Sea Goddess II*. They were built two years before by Norwegian investors, who formed Sea Goddess Cruises and had ambitious plans for as many as six sister ships. Only two were actually built before the new company soon encountered financial difficulties, and so the Cunard charter was arranged. Consequently, beginning in 1986, Cunard had several distinct passenger ship services: the crossings and periodic cruises of the legendary *QE2*; the luxury cruises on the medium-sized *Sagafjord* and *Vistafjord*; the deluxe standards of the intimate *Sea Goddess* twins; and the mass-market cruising of the sisters *Cunard Countess* and *Cunard Princess*. Cunard seemed to be flourishing, and rumors hinted that it would merge or buy out yet other cruise operators. At the time, the company renewed its interest in acquiring Monte Carlo–based Sitmar Cruises and their three liners, two of which were the rebuilt former *Carinthia* and *Sylvania*. Cunard–Sea Goddess, as that division was called, grew in reputation. The market for luxury sailing, with rates beginning at $600–700 a day, was actually expanding. Thoughts were developing on expanding this luxury arm, as well as building a replacement for the *QE2* for delivery in the early 1990s. [*Sea Goddess I*: Built by Wartsila Shipyards, Helsinki, Finland, 1984. 4,200 gross tons; 344 feet long; 58 feet wide. Diesels, twin screw. Service speed 18 knots. 116 all-first-class passengers.]

ROYAL VIKING SUN. In 1994, Cunard expanded their luxury division with the acquisition of another fine name in cruising: Royal Viking Line. Established in 1970, it was the highest rated cruise line of the 1970s, and set the standards for two decades in luxury sea travel. Its three original ships, the *Royal Viking Star, Royal Viking Sky,* and *Royal Viking Sea,* led to an improved, larger version—the *Royal Viking Sun,* commissioned in 1988. By then, however, Royal Viking had been sold to other Norwegian shipowners, the Kloster Group, which owned the Miami-based Norwegian Cruise Lines. The company image soon changed and, by 1994, the *Royal Viking Sun* (seen here arriving in New York in September 1989, **opposite, top**), as well as the Royal Viking name were sold to Cunard. She seemed a good companion to the impeccable standards and high popularity of two other former Norwegian liners, the *Sagafjord* and *Vistafjord.* With this acquisition, the Cunard–Royal Viking arm was formed. Like the other two ships, the *Royal Viking Sun* continued on a largely worldwide pattern, traveling on 14–110 day itineraries. When Cunard was sold to the mighty Carnival Corporation in April 1998, reorganization was inevitable. The *Sagafjord* had been sold off and, by the fall of 1999, the *Royal Viking Sun* was transferred to the luxurious Seabourn Cruise Lines (part of Carnival), and renamed *Seabourn Sun.* Less successful than hoped, by April 2002, the ship was again reassigned within Carnival to the Holland America Line and renamed *Prinsendam.* [Built by Wartsila Shipyards, Turku, Finland, 1988. 37,845 gross tons; 670 feet long; 95 feet wide. Wartsila-Sulzer diesels, twin screw. Service speed 21.5 knots. 760 all-first-class passengers.]

CUNARD CROWN DYNASTY. Seeking to expand into the huge mass-market cruise market, Cunard directors entered into a partnership with Crown Cruise Lines in 1993. The new division started as Cunard-Crown Cruise Lines and included three cruise liners: the *Cunard Crown Monarch,* and the brand new sister ships *Cunard Crown Dynasty* (seen here arriving in New York for the first time in July 1993, **opposite, bottom**) and the *Cunard Crown Jewel.* All handsome, well-appointed ships, they were used mostly for three-, four-, and seven-day cruises to Bermuda, the Caribbean, Eastern Canada, and Alaska. But the project failed to succeed and the three ships were sold off by 1995. The *Cunard Crown Monarch* was sold to Singapore-based operators and renamed *Nautican* and later *Walrus;* the *Cunard Crown Jewel* was sold in 1995 to Malaysian-owned Star Cruises and became the *Superstar Gemini* for Far Eastern service; and the *Cunard Crown Dynasty* joined Majesty Cruise Lines, becoming their *Crown Majesty,* before joining Norwegian Cruise Lines in 1997, who rechristened her *Norwegian Majesty.* She reverted to her original operators, Crown Cruise Lines, in the fall of 1999 and regained her first name, *Crown Dynasty.* Her operations included phases of charter cruising. This was short lived, and the ship was soon bankrupt, out of service, and on the auction block. In November 2001, she joined the Fred Olsen Line, becoming their refitted *Braemar.* [Built by Union Naval de Levante SA, Valencia, Spain, 1993. 19,089 gross tons; 525 feet long; 73 feet wide. Diesels, twin screw. Service speed 19 knots. 916 maximum cruise passengers as built.]

QUEEN MARY 2. The Miami-based Carnival Cruise Lines bought the Cunard Line and its ships in April 1998 for $700 million, and soon announced a very ambitious project: replacing the twenty-nine-year-old QE2 with the largest, most expensive ocean liner of all time. To be later named the *Queen Mary 2,* her construction within five years would cost some $800 million. British shipyards were said to be interested in building the biggest liner of all time, but were actually not serious contenders. They had downsized considerably since the 1960s and '70s, and had lost much of the expertise and technology for such a mighty, schedule-exacting project. The contract went to the French builders Chantiers de l'Atlantique at St. Nazaire, ironically the very same yard that created the *Normandie,* the main rival to the original *Queen Mary* back in the 1930s. Other noted efforts included the liners *Paris, Ile de France, France* (of 1912 and 1962), and a whole fleet of modern cruise ships begun in the 1980s and including the likes of the *Nieuw Amsterdam* (1983), *Sovereign of the Seas, Millennium,* and *Crystal Serenity.* By March 2003, the *Queen Mary 2* took to the water for the first time when she moved from the 4,000-foot-long building dock at St. Nazaire (shown here just weeks before, **below**) and over to the yard's fitting-out berth.

Trials took place in November (*opposite, top*) and delivery to Cunard in December, with a naming ceremony followed by a maiden voyage from Southampton to the Caribbean and Florida soon after. [Built by Chantiers de l'Atlantique, St. Nazaire, France, 2003. 150,000 gross tons; 1,132 feet long; 135 feet wide; 32-foot draft. Combination diesel-gas turbine, quadruple screw. Service speed 30 knots. 2,620 maximum one-class passengers.]

In March 2003, as the *QM2* was moved to the fitting-out berth (*below*), rumors spread that Royal Caribbean International, the second-largest cruise operator, was thinking of ordering a sixth sister of its 142,000-ton, 3,600-passenger *Voyager of the Seas* class—huge cruise liners that were the world's biggest until the *QM2*. However, the sixth ship would be expanded to "at least 155,000 tons" so as to surpass the new Cunarder. In fact, at the time of writing, Royal Caribbean has ordered at least two Ultra-Voyager class ships, due out in 2006–07, at 160,000 tons and nearly 4,000 passengers each. In response, Carnival Cruise Lines is reported to be planning at least two 180,000-ton cruise liners with up to 4,400 beds.

"Originally, Carnival-Cunard were looking into an even bigger ship, one that would be 1,500 feet long," reported Maurizio Eliseo, an Italian maritime historian and author, as well as marine supervisor serving with Cunard at St. Nazaire. "There were limitations at New York as well as Southampton, however, and so she was scaled back to 1,132 feet overall [101 feet longer than the original *Queen Elizabeth*, and 122 feet more the first *Queen Mary*]." Expectedly, the *QM2* is a ship of numerous distinctions. She has, for example, 80,000 light bulbs, twenty-nine lounges, five pools, four embarkation areas, and enough electricity to light all of Southampton. She also has the largest spa ever to go to sea, the biggest dining room and, by evening, her huge buffet area turns into no less than five different restaurants.

Creating the *Queen Mary 2* was a mammoth but very systematic task. The French

shipyard was so proud that they organized a special exhibition about the project at the national maritime museum in Paris. Guided bus tours were arranged at the shipyard, while journalists, photographers, and historians were calling the shipyard offices almost daily with requests and questions. Alone, the hull contains the equivalent of 1,200 miles of welding and has the length of thirty-six London double-decker buses. It was assembled in sections—ninety-four in all—with the heaviest being lifted into her frame at 600 tons. She is big, even by New York harbor standards: she has only six feet to clear the Verrazano-Narrows Bridge at high water and extends into the Hudson beyond the 1,100 feet of Piers 88, 90, and 92.

Overleaf: The *QM2* arrives in the United States for the first time, at Florida's Port Everglades on January 26, 2004.

By 2003, there were some twenty-three liners that were over 100,000 tons. Contemporary ships of 70–80,000 tons seem to be almost ordinary. In fact, the *QE2* had slipped to seventy-ninth place in the current listing of world's largest passenger ships. The first of the current mega-liners was the 73,000-ton *Sovereign of the Seas*, a Royal Caribbean ship that was built in 1988. Carnival Cruise Lines has a set of eight 70,000-tonners (the *Fantasy* class) and six ships over 100,000 tons. It also owns the world's largest combined cruise fleet (over seventy passenger ships in all), has the greatest share of the worldwide cruise vacation trade (nearly 49 percent), and, through Cunard, now owns the world's largest liner as well.

There had been plans for an even bigger ship—the 250,000-ton, 6,000-passenger *World City*—but they have been shelved. Italy's Fincantieri shipyard, which has a near-assembly line for producing big cruise ships, is said to be refitting their building berths so as to handle future liners up to 180,000 tons. So it seems that the race will continue. But for now, the *Queen Mary 2* reigns as the world's mightiest liner, sailing for historic Cunard as the pinnacle of the Carnival fleet. While this book is a salute to her grand predecessors, namely the original *Queen Mary* and *Queen Elizabeth*, it also acknowledges their great successors, the *QE2* and *QM2*.

BIBLIOGRAPHY

Bonsor, N. R. P. North Atlantic Seaway. Prescot, Lancashire: T. St.ephenson & Sons Ltd, 1955.

Braynard, Frank O. *Lives of the Liners*. New York: Cornell Maritime Press, 1947.

Braynard, Frank O. & Miller, William H. *Fifty Famous Liners Vols. 1–5*. Cambridge, England: Patrick Stephens Ltd., 1982–86.

Devol, George (editor). *Ocean & Cruise News (1980–2003)*. Stamford, Connecticut: World Ocean & Cruise Society.

Dunn, Laurence. *Passenger Liners*. Southampton: Adlard Coles Ltd, 1961.

Haws, Duncan. *Merchant Ships: Cunard Line*. Burwash, England: TCL Publications, 1987.

Hutchings, David. QE2: *A Ship for All Seasons*. Southampton: Kingfisher Productions Ltd, 1975.

Johnson, Howard. *The Cunard Story*. London: Whittet Books Ltd., 1987.

Miller, William H. *The Last Atlantic Liners*. London: Conway Maritime Press Ltd., 1985.

———. *Picture History of British Ocean Liners*. Mineola, New York: Dover Publications Inc., 2001.

———. *Picture History of the Cunard Line 1840–1990*. Mineola, New York: Dover Publications Inc., 1991.

———. *Transatlantic Liners 1945–1980*. Newton Abbot, Devon: David & Charles Ltd., 1981.

Official Steamship Guide. New York: Transportation Guides Inc, 1937–63.

Ships Monthly. Burton-on-Trent, Staffordshire: Waterway Productions Ltd, 1982–2003.

Ships & Sailing. Milwaukee, Wisconsin: Kalmbach Publishing Co., 1950–60.

Towline. New York: Moran Towing & Transportation Company, 1950–98.

INDEX OF SHIPS

Many of the ships mentioned in this book have carried different names during their careers.
With a few exceptions, only the name most relevant to the text is reflected in this index.

Alsatia 80
Aluania 9
America 71
Andania 9, 45
Andria 80
Antonia 9
Aquitania 1, 3, 5, 6, 9, 13, 17, 22, 47
Ascania 9, 53, 77
Aurania 9
Ausonia 9

Bayern 14
Berengaria 1, 3, 12, 14, 17
Berlin 53
Bismarck 5, 10
Bremen 3, 15, 17, 22, 26, 30
Britannia 1, 96, 107
Britannic 5, 48, 55, 71, 72, 74, 79, 83

Carmania 1, 3, 92, 94
Caronia 1, 3, 48, 53, 66–71, 83, 85, 92, 105
Carinthia 10, 45, 48, 77, 79, 81, 85, 94, 107
Carpathia 1
Columbus 17
Constitution 71, 85, 90
Conte di Savoia 15, 26, 30
Crystal Serenity 109
Cunard Ambassador 103
Cunard Adventurer 103
Cunard Countess 103, 104, 107
Cunard Crown Dynasty 109
Cunard Crown Jewel 109
Cunard Crown Monarch 109
Cunard Princess 103, 104, 107
Curacoa 43

De Grasse 68

Empress of Britain 17
Empress of Scotland 64

Europa 12, 15, 17, 26, 30

Flandre 57
France 55, 83, 90, 109
Franconia 10, 77, 92, 94

Georgic 72, 74

Homeric 1

Ile de France 17, 53, 109
Imperator 5, 12
Independence 85
Ivernia 48, 77, 79, 92

Laconia 1, 9, 10, 45
Lancastria 9, 45
Laurentic 45
Leonardo da Vinci 85
Liberté 71
Lucania 1
Lusitania 1, 3, 12, 17

Majestic 1, 10, 14
Mauretania 1, 3, 4, 5, 14, 17, 22, 48, 53, 64, 66, 69, 72, 83–84
Media 48, 53, 64, 71, 74, 79, 83
Millennium 109

Nieuw Amsterdam 26, 109
Normandie 10, 12, 15, 17, 22, 25, 26, 30, 35, 37, 38, 109

Olympic 1, 5, 10, 14

Paris 109
Parthia 48, 74, 79, 83

Queen Elizabeth 1, 5, 12, 15, 30–33, 34, 37–44, 48–64, 69, 71, 74, 81–92, 96, 99, 111

Queen Elizabeth 2 1, 68, 88, 96–101, 109, 111
Queen Mary 1, 5, 10, 12, 14, 15–30, 32, 33, 34–44, 47, 48–64, 68, 69, 71, 72, 79, 81–90, 96, 99, 111
Queen Mary 2 1, 96, 99, 109, 111–113
Queen Victoria 1

Rafaello 90
Rex 12, 15, 26, 30
Royal Princess 101
Royal Viking Sun 109

Sagafjord 105, 107
Samaria 9, 77
Saturnia 71
Saxonia 48, 77, 92
Scythia 9, 48, 53, 64, 77
Sea Goddess Twins 107
Sea Venture 85
Seabourn Pride 101
Sovereign of the Seas 109, 111
Stockholm 74
Stratheden 74
Sylvania 48, 77, 79, 85, 94, 107

Titanic 1, 10, 25
Tuscania 21

United States 30, 90

Vaterland 5
Vistafjord 96, 105, 107
Voyager of the Seas 111
Vulcania 38